SELF-COMPOSED

A GUIDE TO WRITING EFFECTIVE MUSIC USING TIBOR SERLY'S "MODUS LASCIVUS"

BY

JERRY BILIK

ISBN: 978-1-312-32660-6

2023-09-07

SELF-COMPOSED

A GUIDE TO WRITING EFFECTIVE MUSIC USING TIBOR SERLY'S "MODUS LASCIVUS"

ABOUT THE AUTHOR

Jerry Bilik (b. 1933), a former member of the music faculty at the University of Michigan, left academia many years ago to pursue a career in "commercial music" – arranging, composing, conducting, and producing music for virtually every medium of entertainment including radio, television, films, recordings, stage, touring shows, and even Las Vegas spectacles!

He began his musical career as third trombone in the Daniel Webster Elementary School Band in New Rochelle, New York, and became devoted to music while attending the National Music Camp at Interlochen, Michigan, where he wrote his first composition at age thirteen. In addition to his musical activities, Mr. Bilik has continued to teach at various institutions, and has enjoyed a second career as writer and director of numerous stage-plays and television productions.

His association with several professional performing organizations and their reactions to much of the contemporary musical material coming their way has led to the creation of this book – an attempt to counteract the apparent scarcity of truly effective NEW compositions in both the classical and popular styles. In this endeavor, Mr. Bilik wishes himself good luck!

ABOUT TIBOR SERLY

Tibor Serly (1901–1978), the author's principal teacher, spent the first part of his life in Hungary, where he studied with Zoltán Kodály and became close friends with Béla Bartók. Returning to the United States in 1925, Serly performed as violist with the Philadelphia and NBC Orchestras. When Bartók came to America, Serly met him at the dock and became his champion, completing several unfinished works including his Third Piano Concerto.

At the same time, Serly had begun work on a contemporary theory of music (Modus Lascivus), which he eventually shared with the author and which became the foundation for this text. Sadly, his life was terminated when he was hit by a London bus on his way to Hungary to receive a state honor.

Hopefully, this book will help establish a valuable musical legacy for this great musician.

TABLE OF CONTENTS

INTRODUCTION 1

CHAPTER ONE "THE GOOD OLD DAYS" 2

CHAPTER TWO THE CHALLENGE 5

CHAPTER THREE HOW MUSIC "WORKS" 8

CHAPTER FOUR ANATOMY LESSON 12

CHAPTER FIVE SOUND ADVICE 16

CHAPTER SIX "HARMONY" 23

CHAPTER SEVEN THE STORY OF MODUS LASCIVUS 26

CHAPTER EIGHT CHORD TONES 32

CHAPTER NINE SIX-NOTE CHORDS 38

CHAPTER TEN SEVEN-NOTE CHORDS 42

CHAPTER ELEVEN WRITING ETUDES 48

CHAPTER TWELVE SUBSIDIARY TONES 53

CHAPTER THIRTEEN "TOGETHER AT LAST!" 57

CHAPTER FOURTEEN "NOW WHAT?" 64

CHAPTER FIFTEEN "SELF-COMPOSED" 67

CODA 73

APPENDIX 1 MODUS CHORD CHARTS 74

APPENDIX 2 BILIK STRING QUARTET SCORE 76

APPENDIX 3 DEDICATION NOTE 85

INTRODUCTION

This book is designed specifically for people interested in writing music, or people interested in teaching and guiding those courageous enough to try it.

Of course, with the appropriate computer program and the touch of a button (or a few buttons) a musical composition can be created digitally, but the approach of this text is to offer a path for creating music in the manner for which it originally came into existence – to make some kind of "connection" between one human and another. As clever as a computer or A.I. program might be, it certainly cannot claim that objective!

The first question is why anybody would WANT to write music? It's really difficult if your aim is to make a genuine human-to-human connection, although not so difficult if your objective is just to turn out something that might generate a few bucks in royalties. If you personally wish to compose with this higher (and noble) aim, or wish to help others achieve that goal, then you've come to the right place! In the following pages, the author will try to suggest specific techniques for putting musical pitches together in such a way that (hopefully) they "resonate" with the person hearing them, and what could be more rewarding?

All music begins and ends in the same place. Someone "hears" a sequence of sounds in their inner ear (otherwise known as the "brain"!), then one either turns those sounds into real vibrations by playing them on some instrument or singing them, or writing them out in a kind of "secret code" that indicates to someone else how <u>they</u> are to make those same vibrations. The process ends when those vibrations are picked up and transmitted to someone else's "inner ear" (otherwise known as THEIR "brain") – what could be simpler?

The catch is whether or not the above process actually "means anything" to the end-user. Anyone can go up to some "musical instrument" and make sounds – even a dog, a monkey or a cat – but it is purposeless as "music" unless the sequence of sounds "says something" to a listener. Music originated as a form of communication, and without that element it becomes simply "sound", so in the following pages we will try to outline some basic ideas for converting "sounds" into "music", or more specifically EFFECTIVE MUSIC!

The success of this endeavor relies on YOU agreeing with the fundamental principle that the one and only measurement of how effective any music is depends on how the LISTENER perceives it. You may think you've created the greatest masterpiece or mega-hit in all of history, but unfortunately, it's not your call – that decision is strictly up to the person hearing it, and that will be the theme of this text.

Finally, the author wishes to add a special shout-out to Mark Clague and Andrew Kuster of the University of Michigan for their generous assistance on this project, and welcomes you to this endeavor as we commence our investigation by returning to...

CHAPTER ONE - "THE GOOD OLD DAYS"

Because of the unusual way music "works" – existing only inside our "craniums" – it seems appropriate that we attempt to trace – very briefly – how music came into existence in the first place. It might be hard to believe, but there was a time not so long ago (in geological terms) when there was no music at all! In fact, there was a time when there were no humans around to make or <u>enjoy</u> music! There were lots and lots of creatures of all sizes and shapes roaming the Earth, but none seemed to have that "natural affinity" for music-making! But then, about 3.2 million years ago somewhere in Africa, a couple of chimpanzees got hooked on standing up and "walking" (as opposed to ambling along with the help of their forearms), and those brave souls led the way to the evolution of the one species that eventually would learn how to "groove on cool sounds" – US!

In November of 1974, a team of scientists was digging in an ancient canyon in Ethiopia looking for fossils when they noticed a small piece of an elbow bone emerging from the soil and realized must have come from a human ancestor. After further careful excavation, the group uncovered more and more skeletal parts from the same spot, eventually collecting more than 40% of the total skeleton, and by examining the relationship of the various bones and the size and shape of the hips, etc., the scientists realized the creature was a female, and also was a BIPED – one of those brand new "upright walkers"!

The "age" of that fossil was determined by using the method known as "carbon dating" which measures the decay of radioactive elements in the soil surrounding it – hence the dating of the find to 3.2 million years ago. Thus it is generally accepted that the skeleton – given the name "Lucy" by the discoverers – was that of the earliest humanoid ever found, making "her" the "grandmother" of our whole human species and paving the way for future concertgoers by the millions!

However, it was the discovery of another upright-walking human fossil determined to have existed 400,000 years AFTER Lucy that provides the major clue as to how and why music actually works within our particular species. That particular fossil (identified as the "Taung Child" after the site in South Africa where it was unearthed), while possessing the bone structure of the upright walkers, proved to have a skull that was greatly enlarged from that of its "grandmother" Lucy. This in turn meant that evolution – even in that short a time-span (geologically speaking) – had granted our earliest ancestors a considerably larger brain – likely for communicative purposes (most species that hunt for food in "groups" have brain cavities larger in proportion to body-size than others, theoretically to support the need for more sophisticated "messaging") – and in the case of the "first humans", that large brain would eventually develop the neurons that would evolve into our unique audio skills, our "tonal memory"!

When we use the term "tonal memory" we are referring to a nexus within our brains specifically devoted to analyzing and evaluating (and remembering when necessary) patterns of vibrations reaching our ears. This device evolved because, once erect, we were a very vulnerable species, and our survival depended on effective communication, so our newly enlarged brains developed neurons capable of understanding the subtleties of our aural signals: *"Watch out! Look over there! Duck!"* The same device within us that implanted a "memory" of what the grunts and hollers of our ancestors meant is how and why we can enjoy music today. Is that cool, or what?!?

As an aside, it is kind of fun to explain why and how that original three-million-year-old fossil we refer to as the grandmother of all humans acquired the name of "Lucy" as the answer is amazingly apropos to our study of MUSIC:

As the scientists sat around their campfire in Africa the evening they made their historic discovery, Donald Johanson – the paleoanthropologist who first found the bones – decided to liven up the proceedings and commenced to play a <u>Beatles</u> audio cassette to add a bit of gaiety to the celebration. You probably won't believe this, but according to the scientist's journals, as the song "Lucy in the Sky with Diamonds" was playing, one of his cohorts suggested calling the "woman" Lucy, and thus history was made!

But enough with Musicology! Harking back to those "good old days" several million years ago, it should be pointed out that it was not only the yells and grunts sending messages to our "inner ear" that stimulated actions or reactions from the brain – it is critical at this point for you to realize that ALL <u>SOUND</u> EXISTS ONLY WITHIN THE "EAR" OF THE LISTENER. A lion roars, a bird chirps, an elephant "trumpets", (a tree falls in the forest) but all they are really doing is setting air-molecules vibrating. The "signals" they are sending only make sense when they are HEARD, and in the human mind those signals and their implied messages would evolve to become the very harbingers of music three million years later!

Incidentally, this observation on the nature of sound also "solves" an age-old philosophical riddle: *"If a tree falls in the forest and nobody is around to hear it, does it make any noise?"* And the answer is simple – NO! Because "noise" (or music, or any "sound") only "exists" if it is "perceived" by somebody or some thing. This characteristic is the essence of understanding why there IS music and needs to be kept in mind as this text progresses.

Philosophy aside, the next important question is how we humans managed to get from grunts and growls and trees falling to the invention of "real music" and the answer to that question is directly relevant to the objective of this book. The oldest known "musical instrument" so far discovered was found in Europe and dated to have existed about 40,000 years ago. It is the bone of some kind of bird into which a number of holes were gouged. That suggests a "player" could blow into one end of the bone and by placing his or her fingers over the holes, or raising them, some kind of variance of pitch could be obtained. But lest we imagine a bunch of Neanderthals sitting around their campfire singing "folksongs" to the accompaniment of their own little "orchestra", perhaps we need to be a bit more pragmatic in assessing just what "early music" actually was.

It's pretty obvious that "sound transmission" from one pre-human to another was an established form of communication, so it's likely that the very earliest "music" was a "decoration" of common sound-patterns heard by our ancestors. It's possible they created "new sounds" with the hope that imitating or extending or altering the sounds around them might impart a "magical power" to them and thereby allow them to offset the fear wrought by the "originators" of those sounds.

Try to imagine yourself back in those "good old days". You and your clan are huddled around a glowing fire in the darkness, and all around you are "roars" and "growls" and "howls" and terrifying bird-calls – all pretty threatening. On top of that, you hear other sounds that come not from any living creature at all but from "some other world"! Imagine how you'd feel sitting there in the dark when you heard the keening wail of wind whistling through the trees (ironically creating sound via the exact same acoustic principle as that of the modern-day flute, but you wouldn't know that way back then!) or other frightening "natural" sounds such as the sound of waves crashing (if near a shoreline), the sound of rockslides or avalanches, the terror induced by the peal of thunder following a heart-stopping flash of lightning, and even the impact of that philosophical tree falling in the forest!

It is not hard to imagine early humans attempting to <u>mimic</u> those harbingers of terror as a means of bolstering their courage in confronting them. Strangely enough, one can find many cases where even today music is used in the same manner – as a device to offset or ameliorate certain fears and feelings. School "Fight Songs" or nations' "National Anthems" are adopted specifically to create a "patriotic energy of unity"; Samuel Barber's exquisite and haunting "Adagio" from his String Quartet created the precise sounds our nation needed to hear as John F. Kennedy's body lay in state in the United States Capitol. Thus, it could well be that the "ancestral flute" described above wasn't used only to imitate birds, but perhaps if one played long sustained tones on it, one might be able to imply a kind of magical quality capable of "controlling" the scary unknowns which abounded at the time.

In other words, from the outset it is quite likely that a "mystical component" was probably assigned to the controlled sound-production that would eventually become "music". It is also quite probable that music emerged in those early days in conjunction with physical body movements undertaken for the same end: to mimic and possibly establish "power" over the motion of trees, birds, animals, and even the "waves" – to get those phenomena "under control". Those movements of course would eventually become "dance".

And what has all this to do with a mega rock-and-roll extravaganza or a formal symphony orchestra concert? Unlike the primitive pottery, sculptured icons, embellished "offerings" to the gods, or drawings and paintings found inside and on the outer walls of caves, music was and is <u>invisible</u>, and therefore more "magical" and more "mysterious". Thus, those new sounds would seem more capable of conveying "hidden powers" over the frightening forces controlling the lives of early humans, and that subtle emotional potential should be in the mind of all those creating music today.

Via musical expression, a writer or a performer can communicate a vast range of thoughts and/or feelings wordlessly – simply by projecting some sort of emotional contour that is (hopefully) perceived by a listener. The sounds being produced go straight into one's brain as a series of perceived "signals", and once there, every individual reacts according to their own implanted memories. Each sound triggers a totally personal and private reaction, and as a result, a well-crafted musical work can generate an amazing amount of emotional affinity in the listener regardless of style or "language", and THAT should be the objective of anyone involved in creating or performing it!

It is the ABSENCE of that effective communicative quality in much of today's music – "serious" and "popular" – that has prompted the creation of this book – a bold attempt to reinvigorate this exceptional art that can bring us together as no other means of communication can. Thus, in these high-tech times of unimaginable technical wizardry, we face the challenge of how new music can reach the listener on an emotional level more effectively – what exactly has to happen?

CHAPTER TWO - THE CHALLENGE

If one is excruciatingly honest, one must admit that in the present era we do not often hear many contemporary examples of classical music, popular music, jazz, or other forms that stimulate a truly effective emotional response in most listeners. We hear "new and different" sounds, we hear "really cool" sounds, we hear "far out" sounds, we hear some really "hip grooves", we hear "messages", we her unalloyed "anger", we hear "gritty beats" and "a rainbow of colors", but how often do we hear something created "today" that is able to generate genuine inner feelings or reactions or impressions that link us emotionally to the writer or performer? Not too often, or at least not in a way that stimulates sympathetic reactions in the listener beyond hearing an occasional "cry of anguish or injustice".

Perhaps, dear reader, you don't agree with the preceding assessment and are thinking of some contemporary piece that really does move you, but does that composition have the same effect on a wide audience? Can you identify present-day "serious" music that generates the same audience reactions elicited by a good performance of a great symphony or concerto? Are there contemporary songs as beloved as the old popular standards? Does Hip-Hop trigger strong emotions beyond shared anger or frustration? Are today's jazz stars truly heard and appreciated at the same level as Satchmo, Ella, Benny, Duke, Monk, Miles, or the Count?

Yes, folks today – younger ones particularly – "get off on the new sounds", but their reactions are primarily <u>physical</u> – ironically going back to the primitive responses of rhythm and movement (dance) from the "good old days" and pretty much devoid of any emotional connection with the ORIGINATOR. On the other hand, thanks to the proliferation of music videos, there does exist a "produced and manufactured" connection to the performer or composer – but again it is more physical or "material" than emotional. That is why this attempt is being made to offer guidance in producing new works – in whatever style – that truly SPEAK to the listener.

From the time of that pre-historic "bird-bone flute" up until the formation of our first "civilization" around 6,000 years ago, there exists little or no information of what might have been transpiring in the world of music, but with the invention of "writing" in that civilization, evidence has been uncovered that reveals music was indeed a factor in everyday life – and not only in the SUMER CIVILIZATION (the first identified civilization in what is now Iraq), but in the four <u>other</u> civilizations that followed closely on its heels: the INDUS CIVILIZATION, in the vicinity of northern India, Pakistan, and Afghanistan; the EGYPTIAN CIVILIZATION, around the Nile River; the MAYAN CIVILIZATION, in Central and South America; and the early CHINESE DYNASTY, located between the Yangtze and Yellow Rivers.

In all of these "new kingdoms", anthropological research has uncovered the presence of various musical instruments such as "lyres" (small hand-held harp-like things), various "horns" and/or "pipes", and an assortment of percussion instruments. In addition, as written symbols multiplied, samples of actual "songs" were discovered which indicated that the art had evolved from simple chanting and yelling to far more precise methods of communicating. Music was here to stay!

It is interesting to note that within these new civilizations the language of music began to "migrate" in much the same way as our ancestors did thousands of years before, and that migration relates directly to the musical language you yourself (or your "student") chooses as their means of expression. Humans who migrated east from Africa embraced a music based on related tones of certain intervals that have carried over to this very day, making it markedly different from that of those who migrated north and west from Africa into what is now Europe. The latter pitch-relationships became the basis of what we "in the business" refer to as "Western Music" – not in the sense of "Country-Western", but music distinguished from that of the lands in the Far East.

This division of styles is quite extreme in terms of pitch relationships, but ironically the two musical languages do kind of "come together" in the folk music of Eastern Europe, such as in Hungary, Romania, Albania, Turkey, Greece, Russia, etc. In those lands, one often finds common "Western" sounds intermingled with more exotic "Eastern" musical idioms. Curiously, this amalgamation of styles did NOT happen in the Western hemisphere, where the indigenous people (who had migrated from Eastern Asia via the land-bridge between Siberia and Alaska) have to this day maintained, via oral traditions (passing on the music from generation to generation), their original Asian musical influences to the exclusion of most "Western" styles.

That "Western" style of music, which is the basis of most recent creative efforts, both classical and popular, evolved out of the great Greek civilization formed around 500 B.C.E., when musical pitches were identified and organized into "modes". For those not already conversant with the term, a "mode" is a group of notes combined together into a kind of "family", and the peculiar tonal relationships of those notes is what makes music in that mode "work" for the listener. The basis of those "modes", thanks to the Greek mathematician Pythagoras, was a mathematical division of an "octave" – the interval in music between a fundamental pitch and its first "overtone" that has been divided into eight steps – with each mode deriving its basic characteristic depending on the distances between each of the eight steps.

As will soon become apparent, those modes will prove of great significance in the creation of effective new works of music based on the principles of Modus Lascivus espoused herein – compositions that could work well regardless of the style chosen – so we all owe a little gratitude to those ancient Greeks for coming up with the idea of modes in the first place!

Now, going back to our story of music's evolution, as we humans multiplied (the one thing we're really, really good at!), the population of Europe began to grow, and as more folks arrived, an interesting amalgam of musical sounds started to evolve as the "populace" carried with them tonal memories of chants, dances, and songs passed on from generation to generation for who-knows-how-long. The result was the gradual formation of a new musical language involving pitches that tended to sort of "lean" in a peculiar way – pitches that tended to "push" the music forward – a new kind of tonal organization in which the notes began to reorganize themselves to establish a sort of an acoustical "home-base", referred to "in the business" as a "tonic" (not like "gin and tonic", but tonic as in the basic "tone" of a piece).

More importantly, as the centuries passed, Western music began to become divided into two distinct parts: On one hand, "traditional music" was embraced by common folk who employed it to amplify the emotions of work, love, death, holidays, etc., and has continued to evolve to this very day as FOLK MUSIC. On the other hand, the Greek modes became part of early Christian worship (as heard in the Gregorian Chants which were widely sung in the 10th and 11th Centuries), and because the Catholic Church was so powerful at the time, it more or less dictated the actual "composition of music" – that is, music specifically "made up" by somebody and written down in an early florid notation (as opposed to the folk music which was mainly passed on through oral traditions).

In the 1360s, the history of music changed when a popular composer (with the Church!), Guillaume de Machaut, became the first human to actually <u>write</u> <u>down</u> an entire "original" Catholic Mass ("Messe de Notre Dame"). While Machaut was obviously not the only person writing new music, that particular work became the catalyst for the "serious" compositions created over the next several centuries.

As time passed, more and more "budding composers" tried their hand at creating original pieces of music, and it was inevitable that eventually, about 300 years after Machaut, some writers in Europe began re-inserting elements of their own country's "folk music" into their original compositions, either setting complete songs, or picking out little "snippets" and reworking them via various repetitions, variations, changes in mode or tempo, etc. to become part of a larger, longer musical structure. This was the guiding principle upon which the great musical "classics" were built, and contrary to what some "advocates of modernism" propound, these concepts have a critical direct bearing on successful new music of any style, as will soon be explained.

Once the floodgates of skillful creative energy were opened, the Western world was exposed to a vast panoply of music – no longer carrying all kinds of mystical magical "charms" but exhibiting fascinating combinations of pitches that were able to intrigue and please listeners. How these "toots", "honks", and "scratches" were able to stir one's emotions is the basis of all music's success, and thus will be fully analyzed in the following chapter.

CHAPTER THREE - HOW MUSIC "WORKS"

All over the world, people go to serious concerts, recitals, rock fests, folk fests, operas, oratorios, jazz extravaganzas, etc., and if one is truly interested, one needs to ask, "why do they go?" especially as in most cases those people have paid good money for the experience! From the outset, the author stressed the critical point that all music exists only "internally" within the listener's mind, but at the same time it must be acknowledged that there are many listeners who couldn't care less about the "quality" of what they're hearing – they just want "distracting sounds" and a distracting experience to help them forget their woes. Nevertheless, "good" music of any style possesses a quality that allows the listener to transcend the mundane and experience a kind of sub-conscious connection with the writer or performer, and that attribute reminds the listener of his or her "place" amid the human throng. Good music connects the listener to the total human spirit like nothing else can.

In some ways, this same observation is true for all "art". Art is our human species' most significant and positive attribute, and its only reason for existence is the opportunity for a listener or a viewer to gain an understanding that something as "useless" as a painting, a poem, a sculpture, or a piece of music affords a total stranger the chance to witness a creative effort by another total stranger and to think, *Why is he or she doing this? He or she is trying to tell me something, so I must observe more closely.* And so, a human-to-human connection is made on a unique level that helps strengthen us as a species as it produces a feeling of "commonality".

THAT feeling is how we humans survived in the first place – not as individuals, but as a group working together. That's why our brains are so large, and for all the "problems" our brains have caused, is not this finer result worth it?

Besides the intrinsic human connection, there is another element present in the appreciation of all art and that is the recognition of BEAUTY. As we struggle through our daily lives, our focus is – by necessity – on "survival": Earning enough compensation to buy sufficient food, clothing, and shelter; doing what it takes to stay healthy and keep one's family healthy; sticking to the "grind". But while we focus inward on the "necessities", on the "outside", all around us are MIRACLES – the miracles of Nature – the living world that surrounds us, the lands and seas of our home planet, the sun, the stars, the myriad life-forms with which we share this place. The sum total of all that REALITY is sheer unequalled BEAUTY, and the accomplished artist strives desperately to capture and remind us of that beauty!

Creating beauty in art is not some haphazard attempt at throwing paint on a canvas or letting a computer work out a musical composition (yes, A.I. can do that!). Achieving real beauty in a "human-made" creation requires exceptional skill and effort and success is not easily obtained (on this, as a composer, I can speak from personal experience!). It is quite depressing to hear someone say, "*I couldn't care less about classical music! It's totally irrelevant – just a bunch of notes written by white men for rich white men and women, or for their churches!*" While that observation is true to some extent, it nevertheless is depressing because it so misses the point about art in the first place.

The reason we humans <u>have</u> art is because of what it represents – an effort to "lift us up", to stimulate some kind of HIGHER SPIRITUAL OR EMOTIONAL INTERCONNECTION between us, and to remind us that within each of us, EVERY ONE OF US, there is a "higher plane" – a place where we surpass the mundane and appreciate the purity of sheer BEAUTY. A work of art – any style of art – is an indicator that the creator of the art (a human) is trying to communicate this "elevation" of concept or idea or feeling in such a way that it triggers a specific reaction in the viewer or listener (another human). It's easy for some to say "*well, some pop tune or rock-and-roll number can never be considered art – it's just DRIVEL!*", but you cannot condemn an entire genre that way. In every style there exists works that transcend and really reach out and "touch" the listener, so just because one is not enamored with a certain style or "language" in an art-form, that is not sufficient reason to dismiss it in totality.

If striving for some artistic merit in any piece of music sounds like poetic dreaming, it might be wise to consider one fact of REALITY: Of all the BILLIONS of creatures inhabiting this spinning globe we call the Earth, only ONE makes and appreciates "art". Why? If the Prime Directive in Nature is "survival", why should something completely irrelevant to survival even exist, much less be a hallmark of only one single species? Those that choose to "pooh-pooh" art are sadly casting themselves downwards and backwards through the evolutionary ladder and that is truly tragic as ramifications of this negative attitude are sadly all too evident in modern society.

The "best" art – in any medium – the art that "moves" the viewer or listener, is usually the result of intense training and effort on the part of the creator, and in most cases involves gaining total familiarity with the particular medium as well as the skills necessary to most effectively manipulate available resources. That of course is the specific objective of this book – to expose the reader to techniques and mindsets that best offer the path to a truly successful musical composition, whether symphony or salsa. Will it be successful? We shall soon see.

Let us return to the subject-at-hand and consider for a moment the "European Composers" – those "old white men" (although Mozart never made it past his thirties!) who many consider "irrelevant" to these modern times, but who nevertheless have produced the vast library of regularly-performed concert works. How strange that some people can reach a state of almost pure ecstasy upon hearing that music while others yawn and sneak a peek at their smartphones. Hopefully, having taken the trouble to peruse this book, you at least have some understanding of the former group, and if that's the case, "Huzzah!" for you!

Now to the matter of "good music" and how it "works": Regardless of your favorite style of expression, it will serve you well if at this point we review the actual mechanism by which all music works. The clue to that "secret" lies within the most significant period in which advanced compositional skills evolved, specifically the years between the late 1600s and the early 1900s. During this time European composers (and some in the Americas as well) developed incredibly sophisticated techniques of exploiting the twelve pitches of the Western musical scale to create aesthetically pleasing SCULPTURES IN TIME – for, in music, "time" is the canvas or the rough stone or the blank page that is the foundation of whatever is created. This observation is as true for jazz and pop music as for the "classics".

As stated at the outset of this text, the most important point in understanding how music works is the fact that, unlike other artistic creations which have a <u>material</u> existence, such as a book, a painting, a statue, or even a building, etc. (in other words once made, they are THERE – somewhere), any musical structure created by a composer and subsequently performed by someone actually has no material existence at all except INSIDE THE MIND of the listener, and the <u>dimensions</u> of that particular experience only existence in TIME!

The skeptic might say, "*Well, WRITTEN or RECORDED music is real and concrete – it actually exists!*" but of course what exists on paper (or on a recording) is only a bunch of dots and lines and dashes (or electronic impulses), so until it is turned into REAL SOUND that is actually HEARD, it's not music at all!

Think back to the challenge discussed in the previous chapter: If you are going to create a musical composition, you have to realize that whoever hears that work must "lend" you a part of their life, whether three minutes, ten minutes, or more than an hour. That listener is going to trust you and the performer to make that devotion of time worthwhile, and that's an awesome responsibility because time is not recoverable – every second that goes by is gone forever!

The great composers from almost every country rose to that challenge by combining the twelve tones into certain perceptible patterns that held the attention of the listener – that guided them along a musical path with a certain form or shape that proved intriguing enough to produce a truly rewarding, uplifting experience. The dimensions of those patterns were in three parts, which evolved historically in the following order: (1.) RHYTHM – the distance IN TIME between one sound and the next – strangely enough perhaps the most powerful element in projecting certain emotions; (2.) MELODY – the succession of one pitch after another – the sequence of tones then delineating a "contour" through time which in turn could suggest an emotional "flow"; and (3.) HARMONY – the simultaneous sounding of various pitches – while the "youngest" element, in some ways harmony can serve as the most powerful "emotional engine", as will be illustrated later.

Obviously, it is the combination of these three elements that constitute all music. Some smarty-pants might say at this point, *"Oh, yeah? I can write a single-line piece so there would be no harmony – Hah!"* Sorry, Bub, but even though there may be no pitches sounding simultaneously, Western music has evolved so far that even a sequence of single pitches can IMPLY a harmonic relationship whether you want it to or not. And, as will become evident much later in this text, trying to eschew "harmony" is like trying to drive an automobile without ever using third gear – just wasting a most valuable asset!

All three elements are major factors in our internal "audio-system" – what I am referring to as our "tonal memory" – that part of every brain that focuses strictly on incoming sounds and stores and interprets the aural patterns received by our ears. Beyond music, tonal memory is how each of us knows who's talking to us, even if we can't see the person (assuming we've heard the voice previously). Sensing this characteristic of human perception, the most accomplished composers all created patterns of sound early in a work specifically to have them implanted in our tonal memory (think of the first four notes of Beethoven's Fifth Symphony: *"DOT/DOT/DOT/DASH - - - — "*). Then they manipulated and varied those patterns to keep us intrigued, and more than that, they created an overriding shape or contour – a true "structure of sound" – which produced a corresponding emotional contour inside us. Pretty clever, right?

As a music-lover (which you must be if you've opened this book!), you know exactly what I am describing, and you can no doubt think of certain songs or classical works that upon hearing them give you a special pleasure. A good song or symphony can produce in each of us the same sensations as a really "cool" amusement-park ride: anticipation, ups and downs, surprises, sudden turns, and ultimately a most satisfying finish. The comment – especially from younger people – that classical music "is *OK but it takes too long*" reveals an inability to really absorb and enjoy a pleasant, rewarding experience, and that's a true tragedy as it reveals a disconnect between their conscious and their subconscious – the part of them that deals with inner feelings and emotions.

Getting younger people to "slow down and enjoy Life" is way beyond the purview of this book, but the potential for emotional connection exists in music, and hopefully this effort may be one meager step towards that goal.

CHAPTER FOUR - ANATOMY LESSON

To best illustrate precisely how music "works", I would like to now present a specific example of a "traditional" serious composition and examine it "anatomically" to reveal exactly how it impacts one's emotions – in this case YOUR emotions! We are going to examine a work by the French composer Maurice Ravel, who is known for his numerous pieces of outstanding beauty and effectiveness. His most popular work by FAR is entitled "Bolero", a composition commissioned by a noted dancer of the time and one which Ravel himself described as rather unimportant – *"fifteen minutes of the same music played by different instruments with as little variation as possible."*

Yet, this "unimportant piece" of Ravel became one of the most popular works in all orchestra literature. Why? How? If you're familiar with the piece, you may be among those who shudder at the thought of hearing it again because it is so "***B-O-R-I-N-G***", but obviously the work is appealing enough to many others that it warrants inclusion on so many programs and on so many recordings. What's going on? What's the secret? The answer is a most important clue to anyone thinking about creating their own piece of music (or guiding someone else to that end), so let's have at it!

Remember, every musical composition begins (and ends) with some musical figure forming inside the creator's head. In the case of a "commissioned work" (somebody asks for a specific piece of music), some thought must be given to what exactly the "patron" is requesting. In this particular instance, the well-known dancer, Ida Rubenstein, wanted music specifically in the dance-form known as the Bolero, and that of course told Ravel exactly what he wanted to know and triggered the entire anatomical outline of the composition!

The dominant feature of the Bolero is its <u>rhythm</u> – the most fundamental of music's three elements. This dance form is based on a repeating pattern of three beats that supports the movements of the dancer(s) and goes something like this: *"<u>Plink</u>! Plunkety-<u>Plink</u>! Plunkety-Plunk ! Plunk! (and back to <u>Plink</u>! – the first beat of the repeating pattern)"* and that rhythm was obviously the first thing Ravel "heard" in his mind. If you are not familiar with "Bolero", you might be well advised to listen to a recording of it at this point as of course the SOUND tells you everything you want to know about what follows!

Given its importance as an element, Ravel started the piece with a single snare-drum (the most "un-pitched" instrument in the orchestra, so all it could project was the rhythm itself) playing that exact pattern. From the opening note until a few measures before the end, all the snare-drummer does is play the same pattern over and over, getting louder and louder (and eventually adding more "plunketies" on the final beats of each pattern), all of which drives the music forward and upward towards its inevitable conclusion. To illustrate the importance of that snare-drum figure, in performances the conductor will often place the drummer in a central position within the ensemble!

If you study the above pattern, you will see how it subtly (and later not so subtly) propels the music forward in that the "plunketies" act like musical "paddles" propelling a canoe. The first "plunkety" kind of gets things going, and the final "Plunks" give the musical canoe a forward THRUST (and "thrust" is a key word in the deeper meaning hidden within the Bolero itself as will soon become clear!). You should further observe that the overall pattern of the "plunketies" forms a larger group of three basic beats, and that sets up Ravel's next creative idea:

The snare-drum provides the basic "push", but Ravel augments that rhythmic feel by adding a bass-note on the three beats within each pattern, and the PITCH of those three bass-notes actually provides further impetus to the forward movement: The first bass-note is the "tonic" or root note of the piece (in this case "C"), while the next two bass-notes are the "fifth" or "dominant" pitch of the C-scale – the note "G" (an octave apart). In conventional music, that precise pattern suggests stability on the first beat, while the second and third beats, like the canoe paddle, suggest a kind of forward "thrust" (harmonically). This motion becomes very obvious when you listen carefully to a recording of the piece.

As the recording reveals, along with the snare-drum, that triple repeating harmonic pattern carries on throughout the piece with more and more instruments added, and with the implied harmonies of the chords filled out "fatter and fatter" as the piece goes on. This gradual but constantly increasing acoustic level and "energy force" resulting from the continuous addition of instruments and the ensuing thicker and thicker harmonic and melodic textures creates a heightened reaction in the listener, which in turn reinforces a significant "hidden message" embedded within this composition – the highly sensual element of "seduction", which is a part of the actual bolero dance.

To further express this secondary dimension, Ravel turns to the nature of the melody itself. Once the original snare-drum pattern has been established, a single flute begins playing that melody – only that one voice, the acoustical opposite of the drum as it is the single instrument in the orchestra most capable of producing the purest fundamental pitch – a pitch basically devoid of "overtones" (harmonics), which we will discuss in great detail later. Clearly, Ravel's intention was to start the dance with the most "innocent" musical depiction (from an emotional standpoint) and let things build from there on out, and build they do!

The very nature of this melody (conceived in two parts labelled "A" and "B" for lack of a better idea!) is directly linked to the "hidden agenda" of the dance as it moves about in sensuous stepwise patterns interrupted only occasionally by some small "leaps". If you think this specific analysis is a "stretch", just go back again and listen to a rendition of the piece. In so doing, you will hear how that undulating melody exactly reflects the motions of the dancers (whether they are present or not) – pretty clever, eh? Ravel also demonstrates his innate sensitivity towards effective musical construction in the way the "B" section of the melody so perfectly "mates" with the "A" section (are you beginning to sense more clearly this underlying "message" of "Bolero"?).

In the "B" section, unlike the "A" section, the melody "arches upward" (get the drift?) to the lowered seventh tone of the scale, and by repeating it adds a new sense of "stress" – all of which is of course playing into the ever-increasing passion implied within the composition. The use of the lowered seventh also suggests the sensuousness of the "jazz" or "blues" feel, and this might be the result of Ravel having met with George Gershwin in the 1920s and being much impressed by the latter's music – so much so that Ravel also included little snippets of the jazz idiom in some of his other works.

Gershwin had travelled to Paris specifically in the hope of taking composition lessons from Ravel (the idea of one getting "coached" by a "master" will be further elaborated upon later in this book), but Ravel refused to take him on, saying the result would be either Gershwin's creative genius being compromised, or worse, Gershwin's music starting to sound like a bad Ravel!

With all the fundamental pieces in place, as the music unwinds, "Bolero" does indeed prove to be nothing more than a series of repetitions of the above patterns over and over and over again, but each time the theme reappears, more and more instruments are added to all three elements with the new instruments also adding more and more pitches – pitches moving in harmony with the melody itself, and pitches "filling out" the accompaniment.

This, by the way, is an ideal example of how a gifted composer uses TIME as a canvas on which to create an effective musical structure – each addition of voices keeps the listener "engaged" and indicates the heightening passion of the dance. By the time one reaches the final melodic repetition, the full orchestra is "wailing away" and producing a powerful, intense sound which culminates in a short final "coda" (a short extra piece tagged on the end) and a massive dissonant chord which swoops down in a sudden descent back to "tonic" (home base!). A "climax" in every sense of the word and one which you would do well to review by listening yet once again!

Some readers may view the above analysis as silly adolescent meanderings and dismiss it as irrelevant, BUT... if "Bolero" is SO repetitious and b-o-r-i-n-g, why has it gained and maintained such worldwide popularity via its purely instrumental performances (*sans danse*)? Because, however it happened, as mentioned above, this composition carries an effective underlying subtext not readily perceived but embedded within the music. Whether you, gentle reader, agree with this conclusion or not, the author guarantees the next time you happen to hear "Bolero" it will sound "different" – and that's a promise!

At any rate, the real purpose of this discourse is to remind you that the essence of EFFECTIVE MUSIC (regardless of "style") is its ability to penetrate directly INSIDE each listener – to trigger internal emotional responses more effectively than all other art-forms. It follows therefore that the elite composers (in any medium) represent levels of tonal and rhythmic manipulative skills which are so advanced they are capable of producing in us a wide variety of emotional impressions just from hearing the sounds and absorbing them, and that is something you should keep in mind as we progress further on this journey.

To drive this awareness home, let us now present an "anatomical analysis" of a typical American "popular song" – a style sometimes eschewed by "aficionados", but as valid an art form as "the classics" or jazz or any other. There are dozens and dozens of truly artistically impressive pop tunes (as they are called), but as a representative example, let us look more closely at one that is likely familiar to people all around the world (and happens to be a favorite of the author!): "Over the Rainbow" from the motion picture *The Wizard of Oz*, composed by Harold Arlen with lyrics by E. Y. Harburg.

Unlike purely instrumental works such as overtures, symphonies, sonatas, suites, etc., music in a "song form" requires first and foremost adherence to communicating the meanings of the words – not only the "sense" of the words, but making sure the melody allows the singer to project the stress of syllables as they are meant to be heard. Whether spoken or sung, there is an implied LYRIC RHYTHM that a composer should be aware of unless he or she wishes to purposely distort those stresses, in which case hopefully there is some logical reason to do so. Most "songs" are usually conventional settings of basic rhyme schemes set to a melody enhancing their inherent rhythm, but others, such as "Over the Rainbow" carry a powerful emotional message as well, and THAT is where the creative artistry of the composer emerges.

In the motion picture, the heroine, Dorothy, is seen in a monochrome setting dreaming of a more "colorful life" in a magical land located over the rainbow, and this of course is the basis of the story. Harold Arlen captures that wistfulness by employing slow rhythmic and melodic (and harmonic) patterns, but he goes much further – creating an emotional framework that amazingly enough appeals to the hidden dreams of most listeners! Once again, if you are not totally familiar with this song, you should first listen to a performance – ideally the original version lifted from *The Wizard of Oz* soundtrack.

The lyrics (words) set the tone perfectly: "*Somewhere over the rainbow, Way up high, There's a land that I heard of Once in a lullaby...*" and the composer sets those words in a melodic framework that is actually a series of ARCS (just like a RAINBOW!) – leaping upward and then, phrase-by-phrase, gently curving back down to earth again. As the verse repeats (with some variation), he repeats the same pattern, re-establishing the aural sense of a rainbow – what could be more appropriate?

Then, to balance "geometrically" the grand arch feel of the first two phrases, he sets the middle lyrics in a totally stable melodic pattern: "*Someday I'll wish upon a star And wake up where the clouds are far Behind me. Where troubles melt like lemon drops, Away above the chimney tops, That's where you'll find me...*". For most of those lyrics Arlen simply alternates between pairs of notes and then soars upward on the final words of each phrase (once again suggesting a "rainbow"), then, in perfect musical form, both lyrics and melody return to the original theme, followed by another repeat of the second "alternating stable theme" which then lovingly soars upward even further, perfectly mirroring Dorothy's wish to go skyward above the rainbow! If by chance the song itself is unfamiliar to you, it is strongly suggested you listen to a recorded performance as all will come immediately clear.

Underlying the melodic effectiveness of "Over the Rainbow" is a harmonic sequence commencing with a tonic chord – "home base" – then a minor harmony (which special relation to tonic will become quite apparent in the latter part of this text!), then a sub-dominant harmony (based on the fourth note of the major scale), then ultimately a dominant feel (fifth note) that resolves back to the tonic. This sequence is significant in that the harmony itself also projects an ARCH – a kind of secondary rainbow! To further bolster the artistic integrity of this exceptional composition, the harmony in the middle section mirrors the more stable feel of the repeating melodic pattern – in other words, all of the musical elements are of a "piece".

One could go further and further into details, but that's not the point. The POINT is that composer and lyricist have combined their technical skills with an emotional sensitivity to create an aural sensation that triggers in the listener a sympathetic response that synchronizes with the hopes and dreams expressed by the singer. THAT IS ART !
And, as stated previously, attempting to guide writers and teachers-of-writers how to obtain that kind of effectiveness in music is the one and only purpose of this book.

To that aim, the "message" of chapters Three and Four is specifically to illustrate as precisely as possible exactly how music "works" so those ideas can be incorporated into new creative endeavors to help ensure their effectiveness. We have reviewed and analyzed two examples of exceptional compositional techniques to demonstrate how a collection of sounds can be assembled in such a way as to penetrate the listener's consciousness (and SUB-consciousness) and provide a satisfying emotional connection. In the following chapter we will undertake one final review of basic musical concepts before moving into a whole new world (not a bad song either!) of how one might approach writing music.

CHAPTER FIVE - SOUND ADVICE

If you are going to compose a piece of music – or if you are going to help someone else compose a piece of music – it is helpful if you have a clear objective in mind right from the start: "*What is the finished product supposed to be, and how do I accomplish that?*" For many writers, the goal is primarily to "get a hit up on the charts" and that entails listening to whatever's trending in a particular genre, then trying to come up with a close (but not too close) imitation. Then, one has to try and find a contact person who knows how to get the piece recorded, streamed, and aired. This type of composing is primarily a business endeavor and "art" or "artistry" play a very small part. If you doubt it, just listen carefully to what's "hot" and see if you can discern any "inspirational elements" beyond pounding grooves and amped-up sounds!

Regardless of the "style" of the music, it is possible, by using creative skills and technical compositional knowledge, to produce something "musically meaningful" in whatever medium you choose. The objective of this book is to present you with a path to creating music that produces a genuine internal emotional response in the listener – not just, "*Wow! Is that LOUD!!*" or "*Oooh, I've never heard a sound like THAT before!*", but something deeper – something that lets the listener make a subtle personal connection with the feelings being expressed by the composer and/or performer. Some cynics might say this is an unrealistic objective, but it's what has kept music alive as an art, and, considering the lack of truly effective music these days (except ironically music composed for motion pictures!), perhaps it's time to try and recapture that magic.

Let us attempt to clarify the process as precisely as possible so that what follows in the ensuing chapters makes total sense.

Why would you (or someone else) WANT to write a piece of music? The best reason is that someone has asked you to (and even better, offered to PAY for it!). The next best reason is that someone or some THING has so inspired you that you feel compelled to express your feelings, and the very nature of music provides the perfect form of communication without having to resort to simple words alone. Whatever the "inspiration", the first thought that must enter the writer's mind is what <u>form</u> the music should take: long, short, simple, complex, large ensemble, solo instrument? And what STYLE: serious, popular, country, jazz, R & B, "sacred", etc.?

If actual words are deemed necessary to get the message across, then obviously the music will be VOCAL in nature – a song, a hymn, a whole opera, a stage musical, or an oratorio – that is the composer's choice, and the controlling factor is how the writer exploits the expressive potential of the human voice to convey the message of the words – whether a solo or ensemble rendition.

Having decided on the nature of the composition (vocal, instrumental, etc., etc.), the matter of style depends greatly on what genre the composer feels most comfortable exploiting. Music these days (and for many years before) has been classified into two primary categories: there is "popular music", basically "music of the people", which is derived from folk-roots and is essentially some variation of the song-form (whether vocal or instrumental), relatively short and concise and traditionally employing easy-to-hear melodic and harmonic sequences. In the present time, a new sub-genre of popular music has emerged – Hip-Hop – in which the totally dominant element is RHYTHM – both in the words themselves and their instrumental accompaniment.

The second primary category is "serious music", which is usually longer and more complex in all elements and is meant to be absorbed "passively" (as opposed to popular music, which often involves physical responses from the listener – clapping, dancing, jumping, swaying, etc.). As illustrated in the preceding chapter, music of either style can be created and performed that can prove very effective emotionally, so the objective for the writer (or the "coach" of the writer) is to determine how to project that extra-special emotional component through just the twelve pitches that are available.

For any writer in any style or genre, the best way to obtain that goal of effectively reaching a listener begins by carefully studying and analyzing other works that have accomplished that objective. Nothing can compare with absorbing the "tricks" that someone else employed to produce an exceptional musical work as it allows YOU (or whomever you are assisting) to "ride on the back" of past successes.

Now, getting down to the "nitty-gritty", as previously mentioned, there are three major elements that comprise all music (plus some minor ones we'll discuss later): Melody; Harmony; and Rhythm. When composing, all three elements should be carefully considered for the assets they represent.

MELODY. In all music everywhere, by far the most important and most critical element is the sequence of pitches assembled in such a way as to reach the listener's ear as a PERCEPTIBLE MELODY. Music began as a single line of chanted or sung sounds, and those patterns of notes have been the primary communicative device from day one up to the present. Think of any "favorite composition" by any composer in any style and the first thing that strikes you is a MELODY – a musical theme (classical or popular) via which your tonal memory identifies the work. It could be four notes or a soaring beautiful arch, but THAT SEQUENCE is the primary messenger of music, and THAT is what anyone attempting to compose must put as their absolute top priority!

Sadly, in so much music of today it is that very element – the MELODY – that is lacking in effective expression (or lacking altogether!) in favor of various "colors" and "effects" and "dramatic gestures", and so, let it be stated right here that "Job One" in creating a truly successful composition in any style is basing it on some meaningful perceptible "good" melody!

And what constitutes a "good" melody? The most effective melodies entail a structure of specific shapes or gestures that suggest some kind of motion or direction, a structure which in turn portrays – believe it or not – an emotional component: Notes going upward suggest "hope" or "happiness" and "light"; notes going downward suggest "peace" and "tranquility", but can also suggest "sadness", "danger", "darkness", etc. Notes near each other in pitch suggest "calm" or "placidity" while notes that are further apart suggest more "drama" or "excitement". Of course, that's an over-simplification, but strangely enough, it all "works" for the listener when properly designed.

In vocal music (music with words) the melody should also be designed to move in such a way that emphasizes the right syllables and the meaning of each line of verse. This is also true of the interior rhythm of a melodic phrase (see more about "rhythm", below) – the notes work best when they mimic the normal rhythm of the spoken words unless they are purposely altered for dramatic emphasis.

HARMONY. While the shape and form of the melodic line serves as the emotional "driving engine" of a composition, the HARMONIES (vertical structures of musical pitches sounding simultaneously) implied by a given melody play a major role in triggering and reinforcing specific emotions in the listener. For example, if you listen again to a recording of "Over the Rainbow" you will hear how the harmonic progression (the sequence of underlying chords) produces an internal feeling of "warmth" or "sympatico"– you actually feel a stronger connection with the performer thanks to the texture surrounding the melody. This is a significant enough factor in effective writing that you really should listen once again and analyze the ACCOMPANIMENT during that recording!

Similarly, within a completely different style of music such as Ravel's "Bolero", it is the constantly repeating <u>harmonic</u> pattern (tonic chord, then inverted tonic chord, then dominant chord) that acts like a musical <u>flywheel</u>, constantly propelling the music forward. And, during the course of the piece, as more instruments are added and the sonority of that harmonic sequence gets more and more filled out, that internal energy increases, reflecting the ever-increasing sensuality of the dance.

One should also be aware of the counterpart to harmony – DISSONANCE – as a critical element in musical expression (groups of notes sounding simultaneously that do NOT blend "pleasantly" are considered "dissonant"!). The following chapter discusses how and why certain harmonic tones "go together", but creatively, there is great expressive potential in utilizing <u>dissonant</u> tones (notes alien to a certain chord) as a device to propel music forward, and remember since TIME is such an essential element in the musical experience, any device that keeps the listener engaged over a time-span is of real value!

Dissonant sounds when emphasized in a composition provide an "easy way" to express "pain" or "sorrow" or even "terror" (listen to some horror movie scores!), but dissonance can also be exploited in a much more positive way: The dissonant sound, within a consonant piece, possesses a kind of "energy" – it tends to want to "lean forward", and that is an ideal device to "push" things onward through time. But more than that, when the pitches of a dissonant structure RESOLVE to a "pleasant" harmonic structure, it produces a subtle feeling of *"Ah! How satisfactory!"* in the listener as can be verified by the tonal memory of most music-students who have been exposed to the basic theory device of a "V-7" CHORD resolving to a "I"!

In truth, there are numerous contemporary composers who LOVE dissonance and just kind of "sit on it" throughout their compositions, whether "classical" in concept, or styled as "modern jazz", or "acid rock" or other modern genres, and apparently there are lots and lots of listeners who "enjoy" that sort of music. This author isn't one of them. I feel the value of music is to UPLIFT THE LISTENER emotionally, and simple devices like the "resolution of dissonance to consonance" is one of the most valuable devices to that end.

So much for melody and harmony. Now let us examine the third major creative element in music – rhythm!

RHYTHM. While rhythm is an obvious primary driver of much of today's popular music (jazz, R & B, rock, Hip-Hop, Blues, etc.) due to so much of its derivation coming from physical movement (dance), in all music, rhythm serves an equally importantly role as an emotional messenger: a faster sequence of notes suggests "excitement" and "energy", while a slower pattern implies "calm" and "rest" and "tranquility". At the same time, elongated variations in rhythmic patterns can provide further emotional signals: music that "speeds up" can easily stimulate increasing excitement in the listener, while music that "slows down" can emphasize calming effects.

One reason the above works so well is that rhythm is the most "visceral" of the musical elements because we EXIST thanks to the rhythmic beating of our heart. That means that unlike the musical elements involving pitch-relationships which we "hear", rhythm can connect all the way to our most innermost essential organ. Thus, a composition based on a rhythmic pulse of approximately 72 beats per minute (normal heartrate) can actually transmit a totally different level of communication, and speeding up or slowing down from that "tempo" can penetrate the listener literally "way down deep inside"!

Besides the obvious manipulations of rhythm in a musical composition, one element that is sometimes overlooked is its ABSENCE. If you really want to emphasize a particular melodic or harmonic "moment" you just "stop the flow" – it's a device called a "hold", or in academic circles, a "fermata", but whatever you call it, it really gets the audience attention! Also, within this category of effective rhythmic "tools" is SILENCE – the total absence of rhythm, and of course, everything else! While silence may seem strange in the context of a composing manual, it is definitely a part of the rhythmic element. Just little snippets of silence between notes (staccato) gives them a "lighter" feel than notes closely connected (legato), and a brief silence between certain musical effects lends much greater emphasis to what follows.

Speaking of silence (an interesting phrase!), in the mid-20th Century, the composer John Cage wrote a composition entitled *4' 33"* that was nothing more than four-and-a-half minutes of silence, complete with a multi-paged musical score instructing the performer not to play anything! While many consider it a "work of amazing creativity" it is hard to imagine how it might have produced a satisfying emotional contour beyond a sort of basic frustration, but as stated at the outset of this text, the FINAL judgement of any musical endeavor lies solely in the hands (or ears) of the listener!

In summary of the above, the most successful music in any style results from the ideal combination of the three basic elements, and THAT should be the objective of anyone attempting to compose, whether the end goal be humble or ambitious. Close behind the "basics" however lies another critical factor in determining how well a piece of music works, and that is designating the INSTRUMENT or instruments required to produce the sounds in the first place, be it the human voice or some "mechanical music-maker". The assigning of instruments to musical elements is known as "orchestration" (whether actually for an "orchestra" or for any other combination), and if improperly employed, it can actually lessen or possibly destroy the effectiveness of a composition, so let us discuss this significant factor as well.

ORCHESTRATION. Music likely originated via a single person intoning a simple sustained sound (or groups of sounds), hoping that its "strangeness" might convey some sort of "magic" to ward off fear or danger. As time passed, the early humans began to alter those sounds, perhaps in imitation of animal sounds, birdcalls, or other natural "aural mysteries" to hopefully generate "increased magical combative powers". Even in today's mechanized and digitized world, a single performer can do wondrous things with just their voice alone: we can make a pitch higher or lower, we can make a pitch longer or shorter, we can make a pitch louder or softer, we can spout out pitches in rhythmic patterns, and we can do any of the above in infinite degrees of variation or combine all of the above into one single "performance" if we so choose!

If you have never been fortunate enough to witness a solo performance by the artist Bobby McFerrin, look him up online and search for him on any digital audio source and prepare to be flabbergasted by what he can do with his voice alone! From his original solo work, he has expanded his unique creativity to include vocal ensembles, but it is the former that is so inspiring – check it out if you want to discover the full potential of the human voice.

As millennia passed and Evolution moved ever onward, innumerable "gadgets" ("musical instruments") of every size shape and type have been developed and incorporated into musical performances, but isn't it ironic that the most effective and expressive instrument for projecting music nevertheless remains our own natural voice? This is supported by the fact that almost every one of those new devices (excluding percussion instruments) was or is an attempt to "improve" or "expand" the expressive capabilities of the human voice, which by default is the standard by which any musical instrument is measured.

The above observation is important as it provides a clue to how one "sets" a piece of music – how one "orchestrates" it. Whichever instruments are chosen should be those that can best project the EMOTIONAL CONTOUR of a specific composition. Many inexperienced composers over-orchestrate their works, thinking they would like "a nice, rich sound" with the result that often the musical elements become obscured simply by "too much noise" or too thick a texture. The "secret" of successful orchestration is strict adherence to the principle that the MUSICAL ELEMENTS and how they are related dominate the sound at all times.

To illustrate this objective, this would be an ideal time to listen once again to a recording of Ravel's "Bolero". While the orchestration expands from a single snare-drum solo to a large full orchestra, the three elements (melody, harmony, and rhythm) remain stunningly clear right up to the final dramatic chord and closing descent. THAT is the perfect example of creative musical artistry paired with sensitive orchestration at every level!

As in the refining of compositional skills, a writer (or teacher) not well-versed in the principles of determining which instruments would best handle which musical figures would do well to find an accomplished arranger or orchestrator to review their scores (or other scores) with them, discussing why such-and-such an instrument was selected for such-and-such a role. While this may seem unrealistic for those not in Los Angeles or New York, one can always go online and try and secure such a connection.

If you hear a contemporary performance that strikes you as particularly effective in terms of instrumental "color", you should try to research who actually did the orchestration and look them up. They may be flattered by your interest and could be an invaluable resource in refining this last phase of the creative process. If pursuing such an exercise seems daunting, keep in mind that the DELIVERY of sound is the ultimate climactic moment of the musical experience because <u>that</u> is what reaches the ear of the listener.

To summarize this chapter dealing with what the author hopes is "Sound Advice", you should do your best to keep all the basic principles described above in mind when attempting an original work. Music composition is not simply a matter of, "*Oh, I'm hearing this real cool sequence of sounds in my head! Let me write out the notes – I can tell it's really going to make a terrific piece!*" If one is truly interested in creating something GOOD as opposed to just creating "something", then one has to consider all of the elements involved, as the correct combination of them is required if the final product is to truly REACH the listener.

Every "creator" should bear in mind that the "end-product-person" is going to lend you a part of their life for the length of your composition, and what they hear has literally got to "resonate" with them – it needs to convey some element of the human experience so that listener can think, "*Yeah! I get it! I can feel what they're feeling – and that is so cool!*"

If a writer or performer creates music solely according to what THEY want to hear, they are short-changing the listener, and it is the author's belief that such an attitude is why there seems to be so little truly effective new music being produced these days. There are plenty of "original works" being performed, recorded and streamed in a wide variety of styles, but how many could accurately be labelled as "inspirational"? How much of that music remains firmly implanted in the listener's tonal memory, or ANY memory? Hopefully, you can discern from this chapter and those following that effective music composition – of any style – requires real familiarity with the medium along with really, <u>really</u> hard work via which you apply every "trick of the trade" to inspire a genuine response in the listener.

It is possible to find contemporary examples of truly effective writing in some of the music being created for motion pictures. For instance, in the "serious" genre of a few years ago, there is John William's haunting violin solo composed for "Schindler's List", and in the "popular" field, the piece that John Legend and Common created for the movie, "Selma". That song, "Glory" is an absolute masterpiece of gospel and rap that accomplishes exactly what it was designed to do, but try and find other popular works, or even "classical" works that can generate those kinds of responses. Not so easy.

But there you are! Perhaps you or your student might be the one to reinvigorate the musical experience in today's terms. It can be done, and in the chapters that follow, a new conceptual approach to dealing with the twelve tones hopefully will offer a path to that end. It still requires the application of careful sensitive thought and "time-management skills" (creating an experience the listener will appreciate), but if one is truly audience-centered, the mission can be accomplished. Good luck to us both!

CHAPTER SIX - "HARMONY"

"Harmony" is usually defined as an orderly or pleasing combination of elements. In that sense, it can be widely applied to many aspects of living: the colors and textures in a room that "blend together harmonically"; the working out of work and travel schedules that "mesh harmonically"; groups of people at a meeting that "get along", creating a "feeling of harmony"; and of course, musical pitches that blend pleasantly. Thus, "harmony" can be seen as a positive factor in our day-to-day existence – in EVERYBODY'S day-to-day existence – because when things are "in synch" or blending together "pleasantly", one has to feel pretty good – right?

In music, harmony has had a pretty rough ride. As mentioned earlier, music began as a single line of pitches projected by a human voice. Forty-thousand years ago (according to carbon-dating) someone came up with that idea of poking little holes in the bone of a bird and making a "flute", and thus was able to make "music" that transcended the limits of the voice. Then, through all the ensuing centuries, music remained primarily just a single-line melody with perhaps some rhythmic decoration, until about 500 years ago when POLYPHONIC (multi-voice) MUSIC appeared. Suddenly, the expressive potential of music expanded as HARMONY – the sounding of multiple pitches at the same time – broadened out and colorized those melodies.

As the years passed, composers began to refine concepts regarding which pitches would sound best with which other pitches, and further, they discovered that a SEQUENCE OF HARMONIES could produce a most satisfying emotional effect in the listener as well. All was going along splendidly in the world of harmony until the end of the 19th Century, when a group of composers (namely Schoenberg, Webern, and Berg, among others) decided that it was time for music to follow a new path – a path that reflected the political, scientific, and psychological upheavals of the era – and proclaimed a NEW concept in which "horizontal equality" replaced the "tyrannical world of vertical harmonies and their relationships" (the quotes are the author's, so don't bother looking them up!).

This new concept had great appeal to many composers, as it replaced the extreme pain of trying to manipulate pitches to engender synchronized emotions in an audience and instead allowed a more "intellectual" approach based on a horizontal sequence of pitches, referred to as a "series" or "tone row". While the "new music" (labelled "dodecaphony" – meaning music of twelve tones) often generated enthusiastic responses from some listeners, in the opinion of this author, these were more an "intellectual appreciation of the pitch-organization" as opposed to any sort of real emotional connection.

In short, it is the author's belief that the most effective means of communicating REAL EMOTIONS in music is via the artistic combining of all <u>three</u> major elements: melody, harmony, and rhythm, and, as stated earlier, the harmonic progression within a composition is in some ways the most powerful device of the three. It is this realization that is the motivation for the exposition soon to follow – the importance and validity of the VERTICAL ELEMENT in effective music, regardless of style.

Innumerable musical works of every type and description are being created every day, and "*Hurrah!*" for the lucky writer who manages to get their work performed and/or recorded from time to time. But how many of these creations actually are able to INSPIRE their audience? How many works send the audience out "humming the tune"? Yes, the "pop works" that are incessantly broadcast and/or streamed do gain a certain "familiarity" via sheer repetition, but even then the reaction seems more "physical" (grooving with the beat) than emotional, and isn't it interesting that so many "show bands", podcasts, and "oldies acts" still rely primarily on tunes created in the last century to be successful? And, in the "longhaired realm" as well, how many "serious" world premieres and important new commissions send audiences rushing out to "buy the album"? Not very many.

If you are old enough, you might remember those "good old days" of the mid-20th Century when people would still buy sheet-music or record albums to preserve the emotional experience they got from hearing a certain piece by a certain artist, so the question remains: how and why has the musical experience – particularly for the younger generation – changed so much over these past seventy or eighty years? What is different?

Of course, the most obvious answer is TECHNOLOGY – amplification, recording, DIGITAL recording, streaming, video, three-D surround sound, etc. Yet, while the "delivery systems" may have changed, it would seem natural to assume that new works, regardless of how they were presented, would still be created that might inspire listeners such as Mozart's "Requiem Mass" did at a concert one summer long, LONG ago, when the then-teenaged author was so completely captivated by the music, he determined THAT would be his career no matter what! If one is truly "clear-eared" one has to admit there is something missing in most new works (again disregarding film music, which seems to retain its strong emotional potential), and it may be the absence of a valid contemporary concept of pitch-organization other than the horizontal serial or "catch-as-catch-can" systems presently still having an influence on composers.

For example, can you identify "new" works in the "serious" genre that affect an audience as positively as Copland's *Appalachian Spring*, Debussy's *Prelude to the Afternoon of a Faun*, Shostakovich's Fifth Symphony, Gershwin's *An American in Paris*, or Respighi's *The Pines of Rome*? In the "popular music world", do people walk out of theaters or concerts these days humming tunes like they did after seeing *South Pacific, My Fair Lady, West Side Story, The Wiz,* or *A Chorus Line*? Do you hear folks walking down the street in the 21st Century singing anything like the "Naa-naa's" from "Hey Jude", or doing their version of "What's Goin' On?" or "Respect"? Not so much.

That is not to say the folks aren't listening to music – certainly the younger generation is "plugged in", but if you watch them closely, you'll see they're kind of "bobbing" to the sounds in their ear-pods rather than recreating the actual "tunes". In other words, they're responding more to the WORDS and the RHYTHM rather than the music itself, and that's kind of sad, because the REAL EMOTIONAL CONTENT in music – its unique communicative trait – comes from the shape and form of the melodies and harmonies and not just the rhythm.

At this point you might be tempted to say, "*Aha! Just what I thought! The author is clearly some old fuddy-duddy desperately trying to hang onto the "good old days" – He just totally doesn't get the new sounds!*" Except for the "fuddy-duddy" part, you would be absolutely correct. Having experienced what "good music" (of any type) can do to a person, I very much wish everyone could share in that wonderful communal experience – not just jumping up and down and waving their arms at a mega rock concert, but sitting quietly and letting the sheer BEAUTY OF SOUND of a well-crafted piece of music permeate one's being.

It is the author's opinion (and that of many others as well) that the dearth of truly emotionally-effective new music is due to the abandonment of a fundamental theory of music caused in part by the "new 20th Century concepts" described earlier. Some will say that the traditional "system" of tonal relationships has NOT been abandoned, but simply "upgraded" and that lots of good "tonal" music is being produced even to this very day. "Good" perhaps, but "great"? Is there a 21st Century equivalent to Bach, Haydn, Mozart, Beethoven, Schumann, Brahms, Gershwin, Copland, etc., etc.?

Consider George Gershwin for a moment. He accomplished something no other composer has done: he blended the musical language of the African Americans with the European traditions of the immigrant homelands and produced nearly a dozen stunning "serious" concert works that are on an artistic par with any masterwork that preceded him. If you don't believe that, it's time to go back to your "listening device" and locate a printed score of any of his major works that you can follow as it plays. In doing so, from his first "Lullaby" for string quartet, to his magnum opus, the opera *Porgy and Bess*, you will find artistic craftsmanship, powerful emotional contours, and perfect compositional form. Still in doubt? Go online and view (and listen to) any rendition of the duet "Bess You is My Woman Now" (from *Porgy and Bess*), and then try and find another that surpasses it musically or emotionally. Not a chance! There are plenty of awesome operatic duets, but none better.

Ironically, the "secret" to Gershwin's unusual success (and remember, while producing all those "serious works", he was churning out one hit after another for his wildly successful Broadway Musicals!) had to do with the very African American music he was incorporating – a music that blended African and European roots which resulted in a kind of MODALITY (a structural form wherein the pitches within a certain "group" work in relationship to the intervals between them) in place of the more formal hieratical "tonal system" normally associated with traditional classical music. That "modality" is the "clue" to the material that is to follow, and its creative significance will soon become clear as the adventure continues!

CHAPTER SEVEN - THE STORY OF MODUS LASCIVUS

"Adventure" is certainly the operative word for what the author experienced in his search for some answers to the dilemma of modern music! In the late 1950s, I was introduced to a gentleman named Tibor Serly by Robert Russell-Bennett, the arranger and orchestrator of all of Rodgers and Hammerstein's musicals and a highly accomplished composer in his own right. Outside of Russell-Bennett's introduction, I knew nothing of Serly except that he happened to live next door to Russell-Bennett's studio on 58th Street and was considered the "musical guru of New York" by all the professional conductors and arrangers in the city.

After a "withering" first lesson in arranging and orchestration (despite the author having already achieved a fairly respectable reputation as such), I realized at once that Serly was a most exceptional musician and was determined to learn what I could from him. As a result, our relationship evolved over the years from student to co-writer, to closest friend as together we probed an amazing contemporary musical theory that, in my opinion (and his) might prove the "salvation" of modern music of all stripes. He named his project "The Theory of Modus Lascivus", and you, gentle reader shall soon learn why!

Tibor Serly was of Hungarian extraction, and beyond his stellar reputation amongst the New York professionals, he was also known as the protégé and later confidant of Béla Bartók. As noted at the outset of this text, it was Serly who completed the score of Bartók's Third Piano Concerto and his Concerto for Viola – the latter especially appropriate as he was also an accomplished professional violist.

It was in this later capacity that Serly began to ask himself questions about where original serious music was going in the mid-20th Century. Was conventional tonality truly finished? Were we indeed entering a new age of music, as propounded by those embracing serial twelve-tone concepts? It was to him – a puzzlement.

His quest for answers began with that very question: *"Were the twelve-tone people correct? Was "conventional music" all used up and no longer relevant?"* To answer that question, Serly began to go back in time and analyze various compositions by the great masters. He soon realized that virtually ALL of them were based on a theory of music first developed by the French composer and theorist Jean-Philippe Rameau (1683–1764) in the early 1700s.

In his analysis, Serly discovered that the major composers, from the 18th through the 20th Century (not counting the "revolutionaries") employed a framework of tonal relationships primarily based on the four triads (major, minor, diminished, and augmented), on a number of "seventh-chords" (triads with another third added on top), and occasionally on one or two "ninth-chords" (chords with yet another third added on top of a seventh-chord).

Serly also observed that as the years went on, composers had moved from a rather strict reliance on those harmonies (albeit with all kinds of passing and melodic tones interwoven), to a more "daring" language employing more and more "chromatics" – tones altered from their normal scale functions through the use of "accidentals" (altering a pitch by writing in a "sharp-sign" or "flat-sign" or other symbol). Nevertheless, when push came to shove, the composers invariably would anchor their works via the standard triadic harmonies – the same triads first described by Rameau so many years before.

Surprisingly enough, there is a logical reason behind the "success" of those triadic-based compositions and it relates to musical <u>acoustics</u> – the science of sound – and to the listener's subconscious reactions to what their ear actually hears when music is performed. To fully understand this principle, we must take a moment to examine the basic relationship of acoustics to any musical presentation.

Every musical "instrument", including the human voice, produces sound by setting some material substance vibrating (except flute-like instruments such as the fife, piccolo, recorder, ocarina, etc., in which only the air itself vibrates via the principle that makes a flag wave). Whenever a sound is produced, the vibrating source (a string, a reed, a metal or wooden bar, a vocal cord, a pair of lips, etc.) reacts to its fundamental vibration with a series of internal physical responses that create secondary vibrations in a mathematical sequence of "halves" and "halves again" and "halves yet again", etc. These secondary vibrations are created by molecular reactions within the vibrating element and always fall into the same proportions of "halves" described above. The exception to this pattern is the flute family because the vibrating source is nothing but AIR, which, lacking substance, is not subject to the division of its vibrating rate.

In the music world, the lowest and most audible vibration produced by an instrument or voice is called the FUNDAMENTAL, and the secondary vibrations described above are called OVERTONES or HARMONICS. As they are produced purely by physical reactions of the vibrating matter, the same sequence of overtones is present in every acoustical sound-generator. Fortunately, while the intervals between overtones are always identical, we are able to recognize one instrument from another (or one voice from another) by WHICH OVERTONES that instrument or voice tends to amplify. Those differences in the strength of certain overtones are the result of what substance is vibrating AND the nature of the instrument itself – which overtones its shape or material tends to amplify or suppress.

The overtones produced by every musical instrument and voice occur in the following ascending order: The first overtone is one octave (eight steps) above the "fundamental" (the actual note being played); the next is a FIFTH above the first overtone; the next a FOURTH above the FIFTH, which turns out to be the fundamental (root note) repeated yet again; then, the fourth overtone is a MAJOR THIRD above that note, followed by a MINOR THIRD as each interval keeps getting smaller and smaller as the mathematical division of "halves" keeps decreasing in size.

The following illustration (Figure 1) shows the sequence described above based on the note "C" because that involves the simplest notation, but the same set of <u>ascending intervals</u> (octave, fifth, fourth, third, etc.) would be generated by any given pitch. In other words, an instrument sounding the pitch "A" would also produce overtones an octave, a fifth, a fourth, a third, etc. above "A" – same intervals, different pitches.

As shown above, there are more overtones continuing upward with the intervals between them getting mathematically smaller and smaller and the sound weaker and weaker, but the IMPORTANT observation (also shown in Figure 1) is that the three most <u>obvious</u> "harmonic pitches" above a root note (fundamental) happen to be the three notes of the MAJOR TRIAD, and might not THAT be a reason listeners generally associate "happy" and "contented" with that particular sound?!?

Some readers may scoff at the above suggestion, but think about the whole history of music and how often a composition ends on or implies the "Tonic Triad". Even selections in a minor mode often resolve ultimately to a single major chord at the end, suggesting via the overtone series that all is indeed "right with the world".

Incidentally, the difference between major and minor tonic triads (or any triad) is based on the interval between the "root" (bass) note and the "third" above it (the middle note of the chord). That is a critical distinction in Modus Lascivus since one can IMPLY major or minor harmonies with just the lower two pitches – you don't need the top pitch, or "fifth".

In his review of the music of the past as well as that of the 20th Century, Tibor Serly asked himself why there appeared to be a LIMIT on the number of basic harmonic structures (chords) employed in traditional compositions, and whether that limit was indeed a valid reason for abandoning "tonality" in favor of the newer radical approaches. As a result, he began examining the structure of each of the chords normally found in conventional music and made a series of significant discoveries:

1. The "essential interval" of any "chord" was the LOWEST THIRD, as it alone determined the "color" of the structure built above it.
2. The four familiar triads (major, minor, augmented, and diminished) represented the full panoply of three-note vertical structures that could be assembled by combining only major or minor thirds.

3. The "seventh-chords" that were also often employed (vertical combinations of THREE major or minor thirds – in other words, another third added on top of the two thirds in a triad) were "problematic" for a number of reasons:

    A.) The additional third, while in harmony with the thirds below, was DISSONANT with the root note! It was either a single whole-step or half-step away and therefore not really "harmonic" (Figure 2).

    Figure 2

    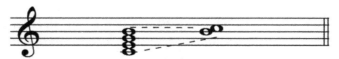

    B.) That inherent dissonance (Figure 2) makes the seventh-chord somewhat "unstable", suggesting it needs to somehow "resolve" to a more stable harmony (to be discussed later).

    C.) In place of the expected EIGHT seventh-chords that should appear by adding a major or minor third to each of the four triads, one discovers only SEVEN chords can be formed because adding a major third above the <u>augmented</u> triad would produce not a dissonance, but a REPLICATION of the root note. The result in this case would be a four-note chord that would still <u>sound</u> like a three-note chord or triad! (Figure 3)

    Figure 3

    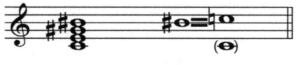

    C Augmented Seventh-Chord   (X)

    D.) Of the remaining seven four-note chords, strangely enough, only FOUR were discovered to be in anything approaching regular usage: the major seventh, the minor seventh, the "dominant seventh" (a major triad with a minor third added above), and the diminished seventh (all minor thirds stacked above the root note – see Figure 4).

Figure 4

MAJOR 7th   MINOR 7th   DOMINANT 7th   DIMINISHED 7th

Serly began to wonder about the above – both the strange phenomenon of one seventh-chord having to be discarded because it duplicated its own root note (Figure 3), and the necessity of indicating the diminished seventh-chord (shown above in Figure 4) via the use of "B-DOUBLE-FLAT". This particular notation is necessary to remain within the principle of writing only THIRDS (and only intervals that SOUND like thirds!). He also wondered why the three remaining seventh-chords not shown above (there should be a total of SEVEN!) were not in more frequent use. To solve this "mystery", Serly decided the best way forward was to examine the guiding principles behind the construction of ALL chords, and specifically why the interval of the THIRD seemed so critical.

At this point some readers might be tempted to say, "*This is getting too esoteric. Any combination of pitches that sound simultaneously is some kind of chord, so why bother?*" The answer is twofold: First, while the preceding statement is true literally, "any" combination of pitches sounding together is not necessarily considered a chord by most musicians if it fails to project some sort of harmonic function. Most would refer to such a grouping as a CLUSTER rather than a "chord", since the latter has a certain inherent sonority based on the pitch-relationships within it. Second, regardless of your particular musical tastes, the vast majority of truly successful music is based on the "pleasant sounds" of notes kind of "blending together" in chords, so it does seem worth exploring why this might be so.

This then was Serly's plan: He would methodically write out every possible combination of major and minor thirds that could be stacked above a root or tonic note and examine the creative qualities of each resulting structure. To keep the system as clear as possible, he would base everything on the note "C" because all Western musical notation is based on the "C Scale" – the seven white keys of a keyboard instrument (see Figure 5, below).

Figure 5

C MAJOR SCALE

In written music, those seven tones are the only notes that do not require any "accidental" (some symbol indicating an alteration of the pitch of a note) or a "key signature" (a group of accidentals at the beginning of a section of music indicating alteration of those pitches throughout the section). Because the "C Scale" was referred to in medieval times as the "lascivious (evil) mode", Serly decided to call his system "Modus Lascivus". And now you know why that strange name exists!

Of course, there is more to the story: As he began creating these chordal structures, a new musical horizon began to unfold – a concept of tonal relationships of almost unlimited creative potential, and this new musical world will be fully revealed in the following pages. The "catch" is that you, dear reader, will need to concentrate quite closely on the ideas presented, since some will involve a severe rethinking of certain musical "norms".

The author must admit that at first I did not fully grasp the significance of Serly's discovery, but thanks to considerable training in music theory, early on I began to realize that he had stumbled upon not just a new system of organizing pitches, but ironically, in my opinion, he had unearthed a system that proved to be THE NATURAL EVOLUTIONARY NEXT STEP IN MUSICAL DEVELOPMENT! Rather than abandoning "harmony" as being "used up" (as did the Dodecaphonists), Serly unknowingly had opened the door to the next obvious expressive phase in music's long development from the Gregorian Chant through the Romantic Era – that of expanding harmony UPWARD!

As will be discovered in the pages that follow, the logical step in moving music forward was not eschewing harmony altogether (as did the "serialists" and other "modernists"), but rather, carrying harmonic relationships to their farthest point of development. In so doing, Serly has revealed an expressive palette of unimaginable dimensions, and, in the author's opinion, THIS is where music should have gone in the early days of 20th Century. Hopefully it's not too late to fully develop this new language and thus present a new "tool" for composers – a tool based on the fundamental logic of the established system that seemed to work so well for so many years.

It is assumed at this point that anyone perusing this text is sufficiently conversant with the basic workings of music, for what follows is quite technical and complex and will only make sense if one fully understands the fundamentals: names of scale-tones and intervals, accidentals, various chordal structures, keys and key-signatures, terms like diatonic, chromatic, and especially ENHARMONIC (that is going to prove very important!), as well as basic musical notation.

As an example, think for a moment about the term "enharmonicism" – a concept that first emerged from the development of the "well-tempered scale" 300 years ago. Enharmonics refers to the idea that a musical pitch could be notated one way but could be utilized within a composition as if notated differently. For instance, a note could be written as "G-Flat" (Figure 6) but could function melodically or harmonically as if it were written "F-Sharp". The pitch is the same, but the notation suggests different functions of that pitch.

Figure 6

Enharmonicism is also responsible for the elimination of the "eighth" four-note chord (described above in Figure 3) because the major seventh atop the augmented triad would be indicated as "B-Sharp" but of course would SOUND as the note "C", thus duplicating the chord's root. Establishing a certain "comfort level" regarding enharmonicism and other musical elements will play a huge role in the eventual successful creative application of Modus Lascivus, and the results will be astounding! Trust me!

In addition to assimilating these mental adjustments regarding notational "peculiarities" in Modus Lascivus, to grasp the true dimensions of this new approach, you will shortly be asked to participate <u>creatively</u> by actually composing tiny musical "miniature etudes" within very specific limitations. The purpose of these etudes is to install in your tonal memory the unique characteristics of each (or many) of the chordal structures which will be presented as this investigation continues.

There is no need to be intimidated or put off by such requests because the "piece" you create is not a test of your imagination or compositional skills, nor should it be considered as heading for the "Top Forty". The exercise is undertaken solely for your own benefit so that you might absorb the SOUND of the basic relationships of a specific set of pitches, and the result of these efforts will play a major role in increasing your understanding of this amazing new theory.

So, now let us journey headlong into the fascinating world of "MODUS LASCIVUS"....

CHAPTER EIGHT - CHORD-TONES

As Tibor Serly began his investigation into this new modal concept and started constructing chords of piled-up thirds. To keep things organized, he determined that every chordal structure would be based on the note "C" for notational clarity, and then he devised a numbering system whereby each "chord" or vertical structure would be identified, as follows:

First, a ROMAN NUMERAL indicating the number of "tones" (notes) in the chord, followed by a hyphen.

Second, an ARABIC NUMERAL, which is either an ODD NUMBER indicating a "major" chord (lowest third major, no accidental) or an EVEN NUMBER indicating a "minor" chord (the lowest third made into a minor interval via the addition of an accidental).

Each subsequent chord number (odd or even) in a given "rank of chords" would increase according to the position of the lowest accidental and the number of accidentals required to form it. Hence, the "first rank" of chords (major and minor thirds only) would be numbered as follows:

Figure 7

II-1   II-2
(major third) (minor third)

*NOTE: To fully understand the import of each Modus structure it's very important that you actually **PLAY** every illustration on a keyboard or other instrument. Absorbing the sounds of each chord will pay major creative dividends as this text progresses.*

The second rank of structures (three-note chords, or "triads") would be numbered thusly:

Chord III-1 = Major Triad (C, E, G)
Chord III-2 = Minor Triad (C, E-FLAT, G)
Chord III-3 = Augmented Triad (C, E, G-SHARP)
Chord III-4 = Diminished Triad (C, E-FLAT, G-FLAT)

Figure 8

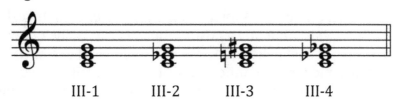

III-1   III-2   III-3   III-4

The third rank – four-note seventh-chords – would be numbered as follows:

Chord IV-1 = Major seventh (C, E, G, B)
Chord IV-2 = Minor-major seventh (C, E-FLAT, G, B)
Chord IV-3 = Dominant seventh (C, E, G, B-FLAT)
Chord IV-4 = Minor seventh (C, E-FLAT, G, B-FLAT)
Chord IV-5 = Augmented seventh (C, E, G-SHARP, B)
Chord IV-6 = Diminished-minor seventh (C, E-FLAT, G-FLAT, B-FLAT)
Chord IV-7 = NOT VALID (see Figure 3 and Figure 9)
Chord IV-8 = Diminished seventh (C, E-FLAT, G-FLAT, B-DOUBLE-FLAT)**

(see Figure 9, below)

Figure 9

IV-1   IV-2   IV-3   IV-4   IV-5   IV-6   IV-8   (IV-7) (X!)

** = If the notation of Chord IV-8 causes raised eyebrows, good! One seldom sees a
C-diminished seventh-chord written this way but rather as C, E-FLAT, F-SHARP, A-NATURAL,
but this notational difference is a crucial distinction in understanding Modus Lascivus, as the
basic premise of Serly's plan is that all the chords being constructed contain ONLY major or
minor thirds. Thus, it's important for clarity that the intervals LOOK like major or minor
thirds! Hence that particular seventh-chord (Chord IV-8) requires the top note to be some
sort of written "B", and since the interval above the "G-Flat" can be either a MAJOR third (B-
FLAT), or a MINOR third, that can only properly be notated as B-DOUBLE-FLAT.

The enharmonic equivalency between "B-Double-Flat" and "A" in the diminished seventh-
chord is the first clue to a critical element of Modus Lascivus. As you explore deeper and
deeper into the system, hopefully you will come to understand that how a note SOUNDS
will prove far more important than how it is written, BUT... how it is written will prove to
be a clue to that note's relationship to other notes, and that also is a major factor in the
inherent logic of Serly's creation. If this seems confusing, have no fear, for all will become
eminently clear as this text progresses.

With the first three ranks of chords thus established, Serly now began an investigation of
the FIVE-NOTE chords, identified commonly as "Ninth-Chords", since the uppermost note
is actually the interval of a ninth above the root-note. Ninth-chords have been used quite
frequently in impressionistic and neo-romantic compositions and are very common in jazz
and popular music as harmonic elements, but, as will soon become apparent, it is not the
full harmonic structure of these chords (or any other chords) that is most important in
Modus Lascivus, it is the harmonic implications found WITHIN each chord!

Before revealing the complete list of chords in this rank, let us examine two five-note-
chords for their internal harmonic potential. Again, considering or playing the full chord as
a single harmonic entity is irrelevant to the ultimate objective of Modus Lascivus, as we will
now demonstrate.

Let us begin with the ninth-chord identified as Chord V-1 (C, E, G, B, D), the major ninth. Let us ignore it as a totality but rather examine its INTERIOR: Chord V-1 is actually a structure of THREE INTERLACED TRIADS – C-Major, E-minor, and G-major (**play them**, please!).

Figure 10

V-1

Because they share "membership" in a single harmonic structure, those three triads are thus naturally "related", and while the C Triad and G triad are the common I and V of a tonal scale, one might not normally consider E-Minor as being so closely related to the other two harmonies, and yet here you are! And as a reminder, while we are illustrating everything here in the "Key of C" for the sake of easy-to-understand notation, all that we shall ultimately discover applies equally to any root note! Everything in Modus Lascivus is totally transposable! The point here is that this triadic revelation is just the first taste of what is to come, and the implications are enormous from a creative standpoint.

To further illustrate how the INTERNAL harmonies within a given chord-structure possess creative potential, let us now examine Chord V-3 (C, E, G, B, D-SHARP) (Figure 11). This structure is exactly the same as Chord V-1 except for the major third at the top replacing the minor third. While there are still three interlocked triads (major, minor, and augmented), this simple "chord" reveals something far more significant: Within a single harmonic structure, a composer can now write parallel major and minor modes and know that they are both logically based on natural pitch relationships. The secret of course is our new friend "enharmonicism" – when employed within a composition, for the sake of clarity you simply rewrite the D-sharp as an E-flat, and lo and behold – C MINOR!

Figure 11

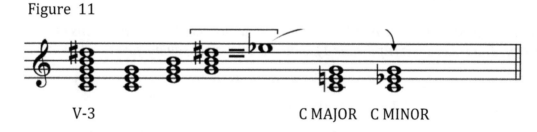

V-3   C MAJOR   C MINOR

As mentioned above, enharmonicism is a crucial concept to grasp when exploring Modus Lascivus. Notes are initially written simply to reveal their tertial (thirds) relationship to each other within a vertical structure, but in a composition, the pitches should be written according to their actual FUNCTION. C-Major and C-Minor are conventionally identified as "parallel major and minor", but Modus relates them to a larger framework – acoustically putting them in the same vertical family and thus allowing unlimited switching from one mode to another while basing everything on a fundamental harmonic logic.

Ironically, this revelation explains via solid music theory why so many jazz and blues tunes constantly veer from minor to major and back, and why that variance "works". It works because, as we are now describing, the two modes are much more closely related than one might expect! It is not just the common root-note, it is the fact that ALL the pitches of both modes are connected vertically.

To hear this relationship "in action", it is suggested you check out a recording of George Gershwin's "Rhapsody in Blue". In the very opening bars (measures), the theme switches effortlessly from minor to major, and this same technique reappears throughout this masterful composition! It all works because the jazz concept is basically "modal", and, as you'll soon discover, exploiting modality may be the panacea for your OWN original compositions or those of friends and acquaintances who might want to compose!

We will return to investigating specific five-note structures shortly, but for now, let us examine the full resources of this particular rank. Just as one potential four-note structure (seventh-chord) had to be discarded because its notation would produce a repetition of a lower tone, so too with the five-note "chords", where one might expect to find FOURTEEN structures (2 × 7 4-note chords), this time TWO chords have to be eliminated for the same reason (see Figure 12, below):

Figure 12

On the other hand, harking back to the "major-minor" pairings within the five-note chords described above, if one examines the structures below ENHARMONICALLY, one will discover additional pairings of major and minor triads within a single structure, as well as additional augmented and diminished triads. Hopefully the implications of all these embedded harmonic relationships will provide a clue to the creative potential of Modus.

NOTE: The chords below are numbered out of sequence due to their positions in the overall scheme of Modus Lascivus (Appendix 1), which is by way of saying, just don't worry about it!

Figure 13 – FIVE-NOTE MODUS "CHORDS"

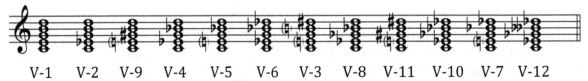

In addition to their melodic and harmonic potential, the 12 structures shown in Figure 13 give rise to an amazing and intriguing "sub-plot" in Serly's investigations: While it's understandable why chords with duplicate notes must be eliminated, the total number of chords in each rank form a mathematical pattern that defies logical explanation: Ignoring for the moment the two original thirds, each rank of chordal structures in Modus Lascivus contains THREE TIMES the number of the rank TWO LEVELS BELOW! Observe!

> FOUR Triads
> SEVEN Seventh-Chords
> TWELVE Ninth-Chords (3×4)
> TWENTY-ONE Eleventh-Chords (coming soon!) (3×7)
> THIRTY-SIX Thirteenth-Chords (on their way!) (3×12)

(if in doubt as to what this represents, you can see ALL the chords in Appendix 1!)

As musicians, we of course have no idea what this mathematical pattern means, but it must mean something! Tibor Serly presented this conundrum to some mathematician friends, but the author is unaware of any logical explanation arising thus far. It is totally irrelevant, but you must admit it's kind of interesting!

As explained previously, the five-note or Ninth-Chords are listed first for the number of tones ("five" shown as "V"), then, if based on a major third, given an odd number, or if based on a minor third, given an even number. The number then ascends according to how many accidentals are required to form the vertical structure and the relative position of the accidentals within each chord. In addition to picking out the triads within each structure, by horizontally realigning the pitches into some sort of SCALE or melodic pattern, each chord in this rank (having five tones) is therefore also a form of PENTATONIC MODE!

As pointed out above, you should **PLAY** all of the triads within these chords AND their resulting "scales" (by realigning the notes diatonically – see Figure 14 for some samples). In so doing, you will discover the variety of colors in each structure, and, as stated previously, this will help establish the SOUND of Modus Lascivus in your tonal memory!

Figure 14

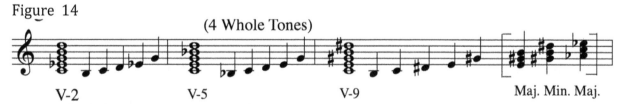

V-2   V-5   V-9   Maj. Min. Maj.

(4 Whole Tones)

If you "messed around" on a keyboard or guitar playing the above samples, and in particular the "chords within the chords" (and of course, in EACH of the structures above there are at least three different triads embedded), you hopefully have begun to realize that some very unusual pitch relationships are emerging – an indication that within Serly's structures a new creative pathway is beginning to open. This is going to become starkly evident in the next few chapters when the essence of Modus Lascivus is revealed.

CHAPTER NINE - SIX-NOTE CHORDS

Right about now it's likely many readers are thinking, "*This is all very interesting, but how is it relevant to composing music? We are seeing a lot of chords and some numerical relationships, but how does that information relate to actual writing?*" An excellent question, and one that is about to be answered in the chapters that follow as we explore the six-note and seven-note chordal structures that arose from Serly's investigation.

Take the six-note chords for example – as purely vertical structures they are of little compositional value since all are rife with dissonant intervals as well as consonant. But think on this: In an earlier chapter, mention was made of the "Twelve-tone Movement" in which the originators put forth the concept of eliminating vertical relationships and replacing them with HORIZONTAL relationships (the "Tone-row"). Suppose, as we did at the end of the previous chapter, we view this particular family of "chords" not as vertical structures, but as <u>horizontal</u> combinations!

What does this mean?

Look at the simplest six-note chord shown below in Figure 15: Chord VI-1 = the "major eleventh" (C-E-G-B-D-F). Vertically, it is interesting because within it one finds not only the same three triads as its five-note relative (plus a FOURTH triad naturally!), but the additional third now provides a true traditional "dominant seventh" V-Chord (G-B-D-F)! That's all well and good for conventional writing, but with this rank of structures in Modus Lascivus we take those six notes and "lay them down on their side", examining their "scale-wise" relationship, and what do we find in this case? A DIATONIC (stepwise) pattern that commences on the pitch "B"!

Figure 15

VI-1   I   V7 I

Play those three chords and the "scale" a few times (ascending and descending). The particular sonic quality of that sequence will prove significant as this process continues.

What the above reveals is that each six-note vertical pattern is also a kind of melodic TONE-ROW utilizing one-half of the chromatic scale (although, in Chord VI-1 all are "natural" notes – requiring no accidentals). However, because the pitches can be used in any order or be combined vertically into any groupings desired, they, by definition, become a MODE. What <u>that</u> means is the six notes of Chord VI-1, by their innate vertical relationship possess an aural "unity" – they are "family" – which in turn means that if used together in a composition there is an acoustical logic "uniting" the pitches.

This is the same principle behind the success of all tonal music – the notes of a given key are actually tied together more closely than one might imagine (as you'll discover in the following chapter!), but the difference in MODUS LASCIVUS is the incredibly broadened expanse of this principle. That potential will become clear as the book progresses.

And now, to the rank of six-note chords!

It's time to test your musical acumen as the following challenge will reveal how well you're absorbing the material thus far presented. Understanding the basic organizational principles behind Modus will prove important when one ultimately tries to compose in this new "language", and it is the author's belief that by the end of this exposition, you, gentle reader, will indeed want to at least "try it out". So…. Take a piece of manuscript paper, or align a couple of musical staffs on a blank sheet, or find a music-writing program on your computer, and attempt the following:

Starting with the chord shown above (Chord VI-1), see how many six-note chords you can construct. The rules are simple:

1. The written notes can only be natural thirds above "C" – C, E, G, B, D, and F.
2. Try to create every possible major or minor third interval amongst those notes by adding appropriate accidentals, but you can NOT add any accidental to the root-note "C" because that simply TRANSPOSES the entire structure up or down one-half step, and that would get you into "accidental notational chaos"! In Modus Lascivus, "C" always remains "natural" (although as repeated previously, every structure in Modus could be transposed if desired without altering any of the relationships).
3. Whatever accidental you insert must result specifically in forming a major or minor THIRD between the upper and lower pitches. That is, it must produce the SOUND of a third and not any kind of second or fourth.
4. You must eliminate any chromatic alteration of a note (such as "B-SHARP") that results in sounding the same pitch as another note in the chord (as obviously it would be a repetition, not an addition!).
5. Double-sharps and double-flats are appropriate as long as the conditions listed above are followed.
6. It is not necessary to number the chords – the only important number is the total structures you can discover (clue: there is one more MINOR structure than MAJOR).

Once the exercise is completed, you can find the "solution" on the chord chart in Appendix 1, but for now, there are so many chords in this category, we shall discuss only a few to illustrate the conversion from vertical to horizontal organization described previously.

As the chords are constructed, you will discover that the six-note "tone-rows" formed by "laying them down on their sides" change dramatically. Some, as shown above (Chord VI-1 in Figure 15) fall into nice diatonic patterns (each note a major or minor second from the other), while others break down into more disjointed patterns, such as Chord VI-7 which is basically (melodically) a series of disconnected half-steps (see Figure 16, below):

Figure 16

Chord VI-14 (Figure 17) is a reverse version of Chord V-3 (Figure 11). Chord V-3, as you might recall, contained the pitches necessary to project simultaneously both C-Major and C-minor as it contained both E-NATURAL and, as its upper note, D-SHARP (heard as E-FLAT). Chord VI-14 projects the same bi-modality but in reverse: The bottom triad is C-MINOR, and the top F-FLAT, as the minor third above D-FLAT of course sounds as an E-NATURAL.

Figure 17

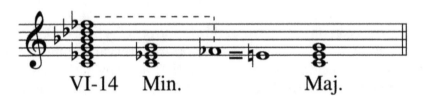

VI-14   Min.   Maj.

Chord VI-15 (Figure 18) is unique in that it produces a "whole-tone" pentatonic scale (with an extra "B" thrown in for "spice"). Again, this is not some idle observation – the emergence of a whole-tone mode from within a vertical structure of related thirds provides a kind of "validation" for such a mode to appear within a larger structure. The more you absorb this re-thinking of pitch relationships (and there's a lot more to come!), the more effective your "new music" should be.

Figure 18

VI-15

The final six-note chord to be analyzed at this time is Chord VI-19 (Figure 19A). Before reading the analysis that follows, examine the chord closely and see if you can discern specific melodic and/or harmonic features that make it unique in this category. This will be a good way to evaluate whether your perception and understanding are becoming more acute. Be aware that ENHARMONICISM will play a role in any successful analysis! To get you started, see if you can observe a similar melodic pattern of chromatic half-steps such as found above in Chord VI-7 (Figure 16).

Figure 19A

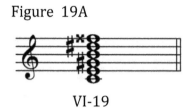

VI-19

Here follows some of the observations hopefully you yourself discerned:

The chord itself contains TWELVE different triads! How many did you find? Remember, you had to incorporate ENHARMONICS to solve the mystery (Figure 19B)! There are three major triads (C, E, and G-SHARP or A-FLAT), three minor triads (C, E, and G-SHARP or A-FLAT), and SIX Augmented triads based on the following roots: C, E, G, G-SHARP [A-FLAT], B, and D-SHARP [E-FLAT]).

Figure 19B

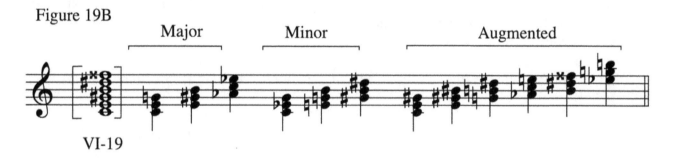

VI-19

The reason for this unusual number is because an augmented triad is "infinite" as it contains only major thirds. That means that any of the three notes can serve as a root, a third, or a fifth, because there is also a major third between the "fifth", and the root of the next octave, as shown below in Figure 20!

Figure 20 - Augmented Triad

The horizontal scale-pattern of Chord VI-19 (the chord-tones realigned melodically) is unique as well thanks to the use of enharmonic equivalents (Figure 21). Depending on where one starts the pattern, the resulting scale is a continuous series of half-steps (the bracketed pitches) separated by a minor third, or a series of minor thirds separated by half-steps! In other words, Chord VI-19 produces an INFINITE melodic pattern similar to the pattern of the augmented triads described above!

Figure 21 – ENHARMONIC EQUIVALENTS

VI-19

If you haven't been intrigued by the material presented thus far, certainly the above observations should pique your interest, especially when one considers that all of these revelations are emerging from a simple organization of related tones into one single vertical structure. And while everything continues to be based solely on "C", once again it should be pointed out that the entire concept of these structures is totally transposable to any fundamental root-note, although notating the pitches involved in such transpositions becomes really, really complicated!

Hopefully, from the above, you are beginning to comprehend that Modus Lascivus just might be the key to an entirely new "universe" of tonal organization and relationships. As this text progresses, you will discover how to creatively exploit these relationships and compose via a contemporary musical language based on a theory as sound as that originally proposed by Rameau so long ago. It may not seem clear at this point, but have a little faith, and let us journey on!

The first real "Moment of Truth" in defining this new endeavor (and there will be others!) will reveal itself in the following chapter as we examine the SEVEN-NOTE STRUCTURES of Modus, the "thirteenth-chords".

CHAPTER TEN - SEVEN-NOTE CHORDS

Regarding these seven-note structures, it should be acknowledged from the outset of this chapter that lots of jazz writers and arrangers DO use seven-note or "thirteenth-chords" as "power sounds" in their natural vertical state, and they really work! But, as stated previously, the most important aspect of Modus Lascivus is understanding that all the "chords" being presented here are NOT necessarily to be viewed as harmonic patterns, but rather as a collection of musical pitches that gain an "affinity" by their relationship within a specific structure.

In the previous chapter, this concept was profusely illustrated as we pointed out the HORIZONTAL or MELODIC qualities inherent within given "chords", and that principle is the overriding message of this chapter. All one has to do is make a cursory examination of Chord VII-1 (Figure 22) and the whole thing becomes crystal clear: Chord VII-1 is nothing more than the C-MAJOR SCALE piled on top of one another as a series of THIRDS!

Figure 22

VII-1

With this rank of seven-note structures, the entire vertical-to-horizontal concept should become glaringly obvious, as ANY of the thirty-six chords in this category can be "knocked over sideways" and be re-constituted as some sort of SCALE.

There is however one further observation to be made about this phenomenon that is quite significant: It is just possible that one of the reasons conventional tonal music "worked" so well for all these years is the fact that the "scale" used in such compositions – the notes involved in a particular "key" – carried an underlying HARMONIC relationship as well as melodic – a subtle unity resulting from each note's "membership" in a single EXTENDED CHORD.

Look again at the illustration above (Figure 22) and think about any piece with which you're familiar that is in the "Key of C" (or in any other key of course, understanding the transposable element of all this!) and how and why it "works" musically. Why is it that all the notes seem to "fit together" aurally? Could it indeed be the fact that those same pitches are related harmonically and melodically at the same time? Hmmmmm.

That dual dimension of pitch relationships is the main point of this text: If the notes in Chord VII-1 sound "unified" when sequenced melodically because of their "membership" in the chord, then the same would be true for each of the thirty-six chords in this category, and in the other categories as well!

As you've seen in the previous chapter, this means that some pretty "unusual scales" or "keys" might be devised and yet possess the same basic unity of sound as our good friend, C-Major! If it works for C Major, why not for everything else?

And if that's not intriguing enough to whet your appetite, here is another observation: Among the seven-note structures, vertical groups of thirds can be constructed that "break down" to form each of the seven major scales containing the note "C": C Major, D-FLAT Major, E-FLAT Major, F Major, G Major, A-FLAT Major, and B-FLAT Major (Figure 23).

Figure 23

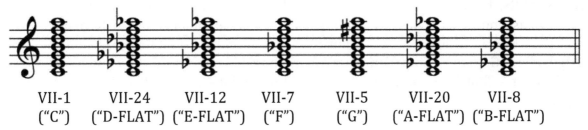

VII-1	VII-24	VII-12	VII-7	VII-5	VII-20	VII-8
("C")	("D-FLAT")	("E-FLAT")	("F")	("G")	("A-FLAT")	("B-FLAT")

Yes! Each of those seven scales or "keys" can be formed from a single "chord" by piling up major and minor thirds above "C", and with that common tone, one can then imply that those same scales, like the tones within them, are all naturally related to each other. If you're adept at music theory, you can also see why those particular keys work so well together in larger compositions – because they all share a natural close <u>harmonic</u> relationship to "C"! Just look again at the list of scales shown above, and this "inter-key" global relationship should make more sense.

If you like mental exercises and have nothing else to do, you might again try to actually construct all thirty-six seven-note chords yourself, but it's a most daunting process. (The author knows this well because he himself helped Serly find some chords he had overlooked!) Just write a treble-clef music staff on a piece of paper, or set one up on your computer, and pencil in thirty-six duplicate versions of Chord VII-1 (shown above). Since every Modus chord employs those seven written notes for the sake of clarity, all you have to do is start adding accidentals to alter each "natural" chord.

The only "rules" in this exercise are the same as for the six-note chords:

1. You can't alter the "root" ("C").
2. You must create only a major or a minor third IN SOUND between any two adjoining notes. And...
3. You cannot introduce an accidental that duplicates another pitch in the chord.

In a way, it's like solving a crossword puzzle, and when you've given up (or completed the exercise successfully), you can cross-check your results with the seven-note rank found in Appendix 1. If you are courageous enough to try this, here is one important clue: Due to the vagaries of notation, you will end up with two more <u>minor</u> seven-note structures than major structures. That is, you should be able to create 17 structures built on the major third, but <u>19</u> structures built on the minor third. Don't ask why, just go for it, don't worry about numbering any chords, and good luck getting to 36!

As in the preceding chapter, at this point we shall select some specific seven-note chords to illustrate their unique properties. As sated previously, the purpose of this exposition is designed to prepare you for actually writing exercises that will ultimately enable you to fully exploit these important internal musical relationships.

Besides the seven major scales contained within the seven-note chords (see Figure 23, above), by default, the same group of chords also contains all the pitches of the common MODAL SCALES. If one starts each scale shown above on "C" rather than its "root", the sequence of ascending intervals duplicates each of the seven modes: Ionian, (C major – Chord VII-1), Dorian (B-FLAT Major – Chord VII-8), Phrygian (A-FLAT Major – Chord VII-20), Lydian (G-Major – Chord VII-5), Mixolydian (F-Major – Chord VII-7), Aeolian (E-FLAT Major – Chord VII-14), and Locrian (D-FLAT Major – Chord VII-28). Here are two examples:

Figure 24

VII-8   (C - Dorian)   VII-5   (C - Lydian)

Again, the point of all this is to emphasize how significant Serly's discovery was in that it provides a sound theoretical basis as to how and why seemingly diverse groups of tones are actually closely related. A musician seldom if ever thinks about any "key" or "scale" or "mode" in a <u>harmonic</u> sense, but Modus Lascivus not only reveals these dual relationships – vertical and horizontal – but more clearly explains why a certain group of notes "sounds OK" to the human ear despite appearing at first glance to be unrelated.

This "natural affinity" between notes within the same structure hopefully will prove a positive influence on you (or someone you know) to aid in the production of a contemporary work with an inherently fundamental logic that can then be transmitted more effectively to the listener. The whole "system" is basically an extension of the same logic that worked so well for the "Old Masters", and its breadth should also be evidence that it can be applied equally to any STYLE of music – classical, folk, jazz, rock, country, world – whatever. If all this still seems confusing, be not dismayed, for we are still at an early stage in our exploration of Modus Lascivus, and there's a lot more information to come.

As stated above, there are thirty-six seven-note (thirteenth) chords. Each one can be reconfigured into some sort of scale or mode while at the same time suggesting all kinds of harmonic or chordal implications between and amongst its member-pitches. Besides the seven major scales and the seven modes described above, one can find several structures that produce various HARMONIC MINOR scales (that is minor scales with an augmented second between the sixth and seventh notes), MELODIC MINOR SCALES (minor scales in which the upper half is a MAJOR scale), and even a complete WHOLE-TONE SCALE (six notes starting on "C" all separated by whole-steps – no half-steps – Chord VII-27). Here are three examples:

Figure 25

VII-4 C HARMONIC MINOR   VII-2 C MELODIC MINOR   VII-27   WHOLE-TONES
(PLUS "B")

In addition to the above, the seven-note chord structures give birth to all sorts of parallel major and minor harmonies (as described previously), all sorts of extreme dissonances (if desired), all sorts of "exotic" patterns and bizarre tonal relationships, and each happily ensconced within a single structure! Most ironic of all, since the whole premise of Modus Lascivus is the logic of chordal harmony (notes a third apart) having a natural acoustical *"raison d'etre"* (reason to exist) stemming from their relationship to the overtone series, there is one seven-note chord that contains the entire set of the most audible overtones, stemming from the note "C" (naturally).

That structure is Chord VII-17 (Figure 26, below), and while its "normal" configuration is the usual pile of thirds (that happens to break down into the F Melodic Minor scale), you can portray the entire lower end of the harmonic series with its member pitches within the notes of that structure: "C", then "C" again (once aligned <u>horizontally</u> of course any note can be repeated – the "rules" only apply to the structures themselves), "G", "C" yet again, "E", "G" again, "B-FLAT", "D", "F" (but in reality, the intervals become slightly smaller and compressed as we go way up, essentially getting a little "out of tune"), and finally "A-FLAT".

Figure 26

VII-17   (F Melodic Minor)   8vb
                                    Fundamental   Overtones

If you **play** those notes in order on a keyboard (or any other instrument), the mathematical relationship of the overtones becomes very clear:

1. First interval – an OCTAVE (largest one)
2. Second interval – a FIFTH (slightly more than half an octave, but that's a tuning thing – ignore)
3. Third interval – a FOURTH (each interval starts to get smaller as one ascends)
4. Fourth interval – a MAJOR THIRD (smaller again)
5. Fifth interval – a MINOR THIRD (smaller yet again)
6. Sixth interval – an out-of-tune MINOR THIRD – almost a MAJOR SECOND (still smaller than previous).
7. Seventh interval (and others) – smaller and smaller (and softer and softer).

As mentioned previously, the primary function of overtones is determining the "quality of sound" of an instrument (or human voice), as each has physical qualities that emphasize or diminish certain "harmonics" (as overtones are also called). All brass instrumentalists know this harmonic series very well as these are the intervals that can be played on any given configuration of any horn – the lower half dozen pitches being quite familiar to listeners as the notes of a "BUGLE CALL". By tightening or loosening the lips, the brass-player can "cue" the proper harmonic, and regardless of which valve or valves are pushed or what the position of a trombone-slide is, the same sequence of overtones will sound – not the same "pitches", but the same sequence of intervals.

But brass instruments are not the only ones dealing with "harmonics". Such notes are very common within the string family, with harps, and with woodwinds as well. In the former two, the player gently puts their finger on a point on a string where it would be vibrating at its fundamental pitch, thus stopping the fundamental from sounding. That point is also a "node" – a point between the vibrations of a given overtone which allows only that overtone to sound – pretty clever, eh?

Overtones in the woodwind family are accessed simply by pressing a key and opening up a "hole" in the instrument where the fundamental would be sounding (kind of like the string-player's finger described above), while in the flutes, overtones can also be accessed by carefully controlling the breath over the air-hole (not easy – not easy at all!).

Returning to "The Big Picture", it should be obvious by now that there is a whole creative musical world embedded within the seven-note chord-structures (as well as the preceding "ranks" of chords!), and the wisest course of action at this point is to select a few structures and analyze ALL of the potential harmonic and melodic patterns that can be drawn from that particular set of pitches. With that information in-hand, the next step is to actually COMPOSE a little short piece of music employing only the notes within that structure.

"What??? Compose Music? Are you kidding? I'm just following all this to try and understand its implications! A Beethoven I definitely am NOT!" Not to worry – a "Beethoven" neither is the author (nor anyone else not NAMED Beethoven!). You needn't be versed in compositional techniques or arranging or orchestration or anything – you just need to sit yourself down at some instrument and try to pick out something musical involving a specific set of pitches belonging to one of the Modus structures as suggested in the following chapter.

The objective has nothing to do with "creating art" – the objective is simply to listen to and absorb the new and different pitch-relationships emerging from the notes you're writing, as all these structures constitute a kind of "new musical language" – a new SOUND – and creating a little "tune" with them lets you absorb the "reality" of this whole experiment!

As you "Mess around" creatively with the notes of a given structure, whatever you come up with will establish sound-patterns within your mind (tonal memory) and make you better able to comprehend more fully what exactly is going on within this new system. More importantly, these first exercises will be of great help in dealing with revelations that are yet to come.

The best part of this miniscule creative endeavor is that you CAN'T FAIL! Whatever you produce will work perfectly to accomplish the primary mission: bringing the actual <u>sounds</u> of Modus into your head. So, "go for it", and good luck!

CHAPTER ELEVEN - WRITING ETUDES

When the author was first exposed to this phase of Modus Lascivus, he was one of a group of seven professional composers and arrangers based in New York City who were taking Tibor Serly's "class". At our weekly meetings, we would be assigned a specific "chord" upon which to create an etude, and the following week each of us would bring in a written-out "score" for either solo piano or some other instrument or combination. Then, in turn, the writer, possibly with help from others, would "perform" the piece and the group would discuss what they heard, examine the manuscripts, and analyze how each of us approached a particular structure.

Since it is assumed that you, dear reader, will attempt to produce these etudes on your own and are likely not involved in a group or class, you have more options at-hand as to how to proceed: You can of course write out a little ditty on a piece of manuscript paper, OR you could go on a computer and create a sound-file (mp3), OR you could just improvise something on a keyboard or any other instrument for that matter. BUT... Whatever you write, you need to RECORD IT somehow so that you can access the SOUND of that effort in the future – that is absolutely imperative!

If you happen to be perusing this text as part of a group or class, then by all means follow the procedure described in the first paragraph above. Rest assured, "quality" or "skill" were never factors in these sessions – it was all about how different folks approached the same organization of pitches – there wasn't and should be any hint of "competition" (and there definitely wasn't in Tibor's studio despite the fact that there was a wide range of reputations present!).

Depending on your own level of "compositional expertise" (or lack of it), for each assignment, you should try to create a little "musical gem" with some perceivable form or shape, or you can just assemble some notes in any desired pattern for a few measures – a "mini-masterpiece" of only six or sixteen bars, or one lasting as long as you wish. While your written exercise should be based on the "C" notation (as are all the "chords"), playing it back on some transposing instrument (like a Trumpet in B-FLAT) will not alter anything since, as stated previously, all of the pitch relationships in Modus are transposable.

In whatever medium you choose to produce your "etudes", the most important aspect of this exercise is actually HEARING it! The goal is for you to link what you're writing to what it SOUNDS like. What it LOOKS like is not important, but what is heard establishes these new pitch relationships in your tonal memory and acclimates you to the whole expanded modal concept that is so integral to this theory. In other words, the whole reason for making etudes is for you to **LISTEN** to them!

There is yet another angle to this assignment: In every instance, the idea is to compose something as far removed from the sound of the "chord" itself as possible. One should do their best to create melodic patterns and possible counterpoint or harmony or dissonance (all limited to the assigned pitches) that explore avenues leading AWAY from the original structures rather than reinforcing them. For example, with a structure such as Chord VII-1 (all the "white notes" – Figure 22), one should explore diatonic (stepwise) and intervallic melodic patterns while looking for dissonant intervals that might resolve, as opposed to writing something that simply emphasizes the triads and thirds of the original "C Major" structure.

The objective of these etudes is getting composers (and theorists) to study and learn as thoroughly as possible what the notes within each structure have to say <u>to</u> <u>each</u> <u>other</u> and then exploit those "leanings" to create new and effective contemporary music. To accomplish this in Serly's studio, each "student" was required to compose their little "Etudes" in whatever style or "language" they chose, but were instructed to only utilize the pitches inherent in any specific vertical structure, and that is exactly what this author is about to ask of YOU!

The catch is, you don't begin writing these etudes using the notes within the final rank of seven-note chords – that's way too easy – since, as stated above, each structure is already some kind of "scale". To fully understand the tonal implications of EVERY NOTE IN EVERY CHORD OF MODUS LASCIVUS, you start writing etudes with Chord II-1 ... THE MAJOR THIRD (Figure 27)!

Figure 27

II-1

Yes, that is the first assignment! What might you create if "C" and "E" were the only two musical tones that ever existed? Insane? Not at all! Ignore the pathetic sample above and use your own imagination to figure out how you might create an actual "piece" by inverting the interval, jumping octaves or sixths, repeating notes, combining them, exploiting various rhythms, etc. It's not going to rise high on the charts, but it will instill a new respect for pitch-relationships unlike any you've had before – even as simple as "C" and "E"! Serly did it, the author did it (a little more interestingly than the above!), and all the clever New York writers did it as well.

When you've completed your first masterpiece, challenge yourself to do the same thing once again with the MINOR THIRD! The irony is that, for some reason, most of the patterns one creates using those pitches seem to want to gravitate (sound-wise) not to the root "C", but to the upper pitch, "E" or "E-FLAT" – not always, but quite often! Apparently, this is due to some sort of "modal implication" that tends to emerge in one's inner ear (brain!).

That realization regarding the natural tendency of notes to feel like they want to "go somewhere" will turn out to be a major clue as you begin writing etudes based on larger and larger vertical structures, and ultimately will assist you in becoming more conscious of the "natural tendencies" of one pitch to go to another. Gaining that skill will have a most positive effect on whatever free form you or your acquaintance might ultimately compose.

Incidentally, the short melodic sample shown above in Figure 27 is not meant to set any kind of "compositional standard" – it was included just in case you might encounter some sort of total creative block: *"What can I possibly do with just two notes?"* Well, that's one avenue that might be explored!

And now, we vastly broaden your creative horizon by suggesting you write NEW etudes using the THREE pitches of the four basic triads (Figure 28)! Once again, the little melodic fragments are included just to stimulate some ideas of how to proceed – you should try and expand your own etudes quite a bit further, and remember, the whole idea is to PLAY each etude and ABSORB the sounds!

Figure 28

While these etudes should prove slightly easier to construct than the two-note etudes, one must be careful, particularly when dealing with the C-MAJOR triad, to avoid writing something that sounds like a BUGLE-CALL! On the other hand, attempting to <u>overcome</u> that challenge makes it all worth the effort from a creative standpoint. Again, the objective in writing these etudes is not "beauty" or "great art"; the idea is to try and mine whatever natural melodic and harmonic patterns you can glean from the three pitches. And remember, as shown in the little illustrations, you can alter any pitch enharmonically with accidentals to make relationships clearer. It's not easy, but it's a great creative exercise.

Once you surmount the three-note challenge, things get considerably easier, as all but one of the <u>four-note structures</u> (seventh-chords) contain a diatonic (stepwise) interval of a major or minor second, which is formed by inverting the seventh. The "outrider" is the Diminished Seventh Chord (Chord IV-8) which contains only minor thirds and thus presents a real challenge melodically. At any rate, it is recommended you create one etude on the regular major seventh-chord (Chord IV-1) to "get your feet wet", and then pick one or more of the other structures (see Figure 9, above) for the source of an etude which you should find more "fertile" melodically. Keep in mind, the objective is not form or style but simply discerning inherent melodic and harmonic relationships between the pitches of each chord.

And remember the Golden Rule: PLAY and LISTEN to each etude!

The melodic and expressive potential increases even further when you approach the FIVE-NOTE CHORDS (see Figure 13, above). By now, you should be able to create much more interesting melodies in your etudes while also implying different harmonic support (suggesting "chords" through the use of other thirds). Again, it is recommended that you start with one or more of the "simplest" structures (minimal accidentals) and then explore a few of the more complex examples. To repeat, the objective in these etudes is not "great art" – the objective is establishing the tonal language of Modus in your mind. That's why it's critical that whatever you write, you (or somebody else) sit down and **PLAY** it! It's not about good or bad – it's about the language of the sounds.

As your production of etudes continues, by the time you encounter the SIX-NOTE CHORDS (shown in Appendix 1), you will think you've reached a creative NIRVANA because that added sixth tone opens up all kinds of new melodic possibilities as well as all kinds of HARMONIC (accompanimental) possibilities. Since these structures project a variety of MODAL possibilities as well as the opportunity for more DISSONANCE, your expressive range should expand exponentially at this level.

Speaking of dissonance, that element is especially important in Modus because dissonant intervals have the advantage of "working better" musically (being received better by a listener) because of their innate "consonant" relationship to neighboring notes in a given chordal structure. In fact, this inherent tonal versatility (diatonic, harmonic, modal, dissonant, etc.) is one of the reasons Modus Lascivus does indeed seem like the appropriate "evolutionary answer" to music's ongoing development, since it doesn't "constrain" the composer but in fact opens up a much wider musical horizon.

Obviously, the ultimate "style" of whatever etude one chooses to write will be the consequence of that person's own musical tastes. In Serly's New York class, each week the etudes spanned the full range of styles according to who was writing them. There were "jingle-style" etudes from the jingle writers (a "jingle" being a "musical spot-ad" for some product), jazz-style samples from that group, quasi-dramatic film-score style from a few versed in that genre, "pop" style from one who had two hits on the charts at the time, and etudes in a "serious classical" style from those of us with that background. And the irony? With very few exceptions, THEY ALL WORKED! – a true testimony not just to the skill of the writers, but to the potential of Modus.

Now it's YOUR turn! Go to Appendix 1, select a few six-note chords, and see what you can produce. By this time, having written a few etudes in the lower chord-ranks, you should have gotten acclimated to the process: (1.) find an interesting chord-structure; (2.) analyze potential melodic patterns embedded within it; (3.) analyze potential harmonic patterns; (4.) create a musical statement in your chosen style of expression; (5.) then **PLAY** it, and listen carefully to what you have created – that's the secret!

Remember, it's not about ART – it's about SOUND!

Once you've matriculated from "undergraduate school" (!!!), you're now ready for the "Big Time" – the SEVEN-NOTE CHORDS! There, sitting right before your eyes (in Appendix 1) are SEVEN MAJOR SCALES, SEVEN MINOR SCALES, SEVEN MODAL SCALES, and who knows what else?!?

But "taking the easy route" is not the objective – anyone can write a piece in C Major! If you happen to choose that particular chord for your etude, your goal should be to write a piece that doesn't SOUND like C Major at all! In fact, the goal should be to see how far AWAY from the sound of "C" you can get! And why? Because thinking AWAY from the "obvious" is how you discover the full scope of pitch relationships embedded in these structures, and those new avenues are the route to creating music that is based on the same sound logic as Bach and Beethoven but sounds completely new and refreshing. How exciting!

There are thirty-six seven-note structures, ranging from those containing the obvious "keys" and "modes" to those patterns that defy easy classification. Ideally, you should create at least one etude in each category (major, minor, diminished, augmented, and "irregular" – a chordal structure that doesn't suggest any "normal" pitch-organization), and remember, it's irrelevant what your etude LOOKS like – everything depends on what it SOUNDS like! THAT is how you learn to write in Modus!

You will find all the seven-note structures on the master chord-chart in Appendix 1, and remember, ENHARMONICS can come into play whenever it seems appropriate!

When you've written all that you can write up to this point, and have HEARD the results, it will be time to move on to "Phase Two" of this endeavor, and what a surprise awaits! (But no peeking – stay with the program for now!)

CHAPTER TWELVE - SUBSIDIARY TONES

We have now completed "Phase One" of our introduction to Tibor Serly's "Modus Lascivus". We have explored how he first decided to pursue this investigation and how he began creating and assembling the vertical structures, ultimately reaching a total of EIGHTY-TWO chords! We have also reviewed how he led his students through an exploration of the melodic, modal, and harmonic potential within the chords while at the same time revealing various broader relationships such as groups of scales, groups of modes, exotic configurations, etc., all of which naturally emerged from the vertical organization of pitches by thirds.

In addition, we have tried to help you absorb the SOUNDS of these new relationships by creating little <u>etudes</u> with the objective of HEARING how the pitches within Modus relate to each other, and in so doing hope that you have now attained some grasp of what this is all about. And what it is about is discovering the next evolutionary step in musical development, the step that SHOULD have been followed over 100 years ago. In place of the proposed "abandonment of harmony" popular at the time, composers and theorists ideally should have investigated and embraced the vertical expansion of harmony, and from it discovered, as Serly did, the equivalent of Modus!

There may be those who disagree with the above assessment, and that's fine – "*chacun à son goût*" – but we still have a long way to go down this new creative path, so let us move on to the next phase of Modus Lascivus in which the musical palette is about to expand exponentially – the presentation of the SUBSIDIARY TONES.

And what are subsidiary tones? Read on!

We have traced very thoroughly how the eighty-two "chords" of Modus evolved, commencing with the major and minor thirds and adding more major or minor thirds on top until we reached vertical structures of seven tones. After combining those seven tones, were we to add <u>additional</u> thirds as might seem the logical next step, we would by necessity be introducing CHROMATIC ALTERATIONS of the tones already present, and that would be a problem as we would have to write two versions of the same note. That prospect would defeat the purpose of mining the NATURAL POTENTIAL present within each structure (see Figure 29A, below).

Figure 29A

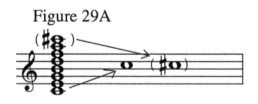

Speaking of "potential", within those eighty-two structures we have identified all kinds of interesting melodic, modal, and harmonic relationships, all supported by NATURAL acoustical properties – and that's the key factor underlying this whole endeavor!

Now we address for the first time the "Elephant in the Room" – the remaining chromatic pitches NOT in a given chordal structure! There are of course TWELVE pitches that form the basis of all "Western" music – the result of dividing the distance between the fundamental pitch and its first overtone (the "octave") into twelve equal parts. Since vertical structures built on the interval of thirds cannot exceed seven tones (because, as shown above, an "eighth tone" would be equivalent to ALTERING one of the seven lower tones), then, for every chordal assembly, there remain at least FIVE additional pitches unaccounted for! Hmmmmm, most interesting!

To distinguish the "left-over" pitches from those involved in the chordal structures, Serly identified them as SUBSIDIARY TONES, or "Sub-tones", and, as he thought about them, a curious idea emerged in his fertile mind: Since the pitches within each chord are all related by their shared harmonic commonality, then the subsidiary tones – those NOT in the chord – by default, must also share a common relationship.

Thus, the next step in his complex investigation involved exploring the tonal and harmonic relationships of each separate group of subsidiary or sub-tones. (**NOTE: The term "sub-tone" in "normal" musical usage, refers to a pitch produced by certain instruments such as carillon bells which sounds BELOW the fundamental pitch of an overtone series. It is a common physical phenomenon and only mentioned here to make it clear that in THIS book, "sub-tone" is just shorthand for "subsidiary tone".**) To accomplish this next phase of study, Serly and his students proceeded to create "etudes" in the same manner as previously, but this time exploring what each group of sub-tones might have to offer creatively.

In this case, the challenge increased in reverse order: The "easiest" sub-tone sources to explore arose from those "left over" from the two-note chord structures – the major or minor thirds. With those two structures one finds a collection of TEN TONES affording all kinds of melodic, modal, chromatic, and harmonic possibilities. Just look at the sub-tones for Chord II-2, the minor third (all the chromatic pitches that are NOT "C" or "E-FLAT"):

Figure 29B

While it's obvious that numerous triadic relationships can be constructed from within this group, Serly made no attempt to try and re-form larger tertial structures from the sub-tones because their <u>exclusion</u> from the "chords" provided its own organization. In addition, it is possible that vertical combinations of sub-tones might result in transposed versions of already-established "chord tone-structures" thus creating all kinds of confusion! To emphasize the difference between chord-tones and sub-tones, he always displayed the latter MELODICALLY (horizontally) and never vertically (see Figure 29B, above).

For the sake of further development of your own "ear for Modus", you should now attempt to create yet another etude using only the ten tones shown above. You could easily create a lovely little "children's song" given all the potential pitches and their harmonic implications, OR… far better, you might try and see how "far out" a sound you could establish utilizing those same notes – it's strictly up to you. BUT… whichever path you follow, be sure to **PLAY** whatever etude you create, because once again it will attune your tonal memory to a new and different dimension of Modus Lascivus.

As one moves UP the ladder of chord-tone-structures, with each rank, one loses another sub-tone, and it is very useful to create at least one etude for each category to absorb the gradually diminishing expressive potential of each group. In this phase, the most important group of chords and sub-tones is the rank of twenty-one SIX-NOTE STRUCTURES (see Appendix 1) for the obvious reason that the chromatic scale is now equally divided in <u>half</u>, and that equality of the two groups (chord-tones, and sub-tones) produces an amazing expressive potential which we will investigate more fully in "Phase Three", the following chapter.

To fully appreciate the creative potential of the subsidiary tones emerging from the six-note structures, you should try and compose a number of short etudes using only those pitches. The most beneficial approach is the same as described earlier: write one or two etudes using "simple" sets of sub-tones, then challenge yourself to create something using a set that appears to have very limited potential. Keep in mind that however you combine them, those subsidiary tones have the same "family orientation" as the original chord-tones by their very exclusion from the chord, so there's really no limit on where you might go creatively! As a starter, notice the "pentatonic black-key potential" (plus an "A") of the subsidiary tones emerging from Chord VI-1 (Figure 30).

Figure 30

Upon completion, remember to **PLAY** the etudes you create and let the sounds permeate your thinking so that they might be recalled if and when you should decide to try some more extended writing.

Speaking of extended writing, the final rank of chords, the SEVEN-NOTE STRUCTURES, produce the most challenging group of sub-tones with which to compose since only five are available at a time, but it is to your great advantage to attempt etudes for as many as you can. As mentioned previously, you can view all the seven-note structures in Appendix 1 and select a few whose sub-tones might appeal to you.

Interestingly, the sub-tones of Chord VII-1 (Figure 31), like Chord VI-1 (Figure 30) turn out to be those produced by the five "black-keys" on a keyboard – in this case, the pure PENTATONIC SCALE! That would be a useful combination were you to try and produce some "Asian-sounding" etude, but the real challenge would be to see how "Un-Asian" an etude you could create with those five pitches. THAT'S the whole idea of all this effort – to encourage you to be as original and creative as you can be (but remember to always **PLAY** what you write)!

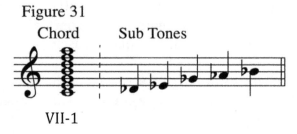

Figure 31

Incidentally, as a wild and fun-filled diversion regarding the sub-tones of Chord VII-1, consider getting yourself a soft-ball sized NERF-BALL (or larger) and then go to some keyboard and press down the "sustain" pedal. Next, take the nerf-ball and just roll it up and down the keyboard on the black-keys only. The result is a truly impressive display of "sub-tones" that creates the illusion you've written the ultimate pentatonic concerto to end all concertos! It means nothing, but it's really fun, and greatly impresses any listener!

Because they are presented as being kind of "left-overs", the subsidiary tones have a slight "image problem", but in truth their lack of vertical organization allows for much more imaginative usage, particularly regarding the element of dissonance. You can take a certain group of sub-tones and project extreme "modernity" with them, but unlike the wild "do-whatever you want" philosophy of some contemporary compositional styles, there remains in this case an inherent organization to the tones (arising from their "derivation" from some "chord") that makes even the wildest sounds strangely "palatable" to the listener, and that's what music should be about!.

You can prove this thesis by selecting any group of sub-tones and combining them in the most "modern" style you can imagine. If you then structure your "etude" with some fundamental logic (form), you will be surprised at how much more "accessible" even dissonant modern sounds can be when they are based on the logical foundation of Modus.

Pick your poison and see what you can do!

CHAPTER THIRTEEN - "TOGETHER AT LAST !"

The creative potential of Modus Lascivus should have become fairly apparent to you by now. First, there are all the possible ramifications employing just "chord-tones" – particularly those within the six- and seven-note structures – from conventional scales and harmonies to all sorts of modal relationships and beyond. Hopefully, via the creation of your own little "etudes", you should have been able to evaluate to some extent the "palette of possibilities" that is available from that source.

Second, there are the similar if descending potentials of each chord's "subsidiary tones", the remainder of the chromatic scale not present in a given vertical structure. In every case, the creative emphasis should be on the horizontal or melodic qualities of a particular set of pitches with vertical or harmonic relationships added for support.

Given the number of "chords" (82) generating all these "groupings", it is easy to see how wide an expressive expanse can be produced – all based on the single note "C"! But now, as we come to "Phase Three" of our learning process, we are going to find that the creative potential outlined above is about to be expanded by THE FACTOR OF <u>THREE</u> (and why not? – the whole principle of Modus is based on THIRDS!)!

Thus far, our study has been focused on the potential of a single group of notes associated with a specific vertical structure: one group within the structure itself (the "chord-tones"), and the other group the remaining pitches NOT in the "chord" (the "subsidiary tones"). Now we are about to enter our final phase in which we look at the creative potential arising from COMBINING the two separate groups!

What does this mean? We have one set of pitches that are related by their presence in a "chord", and a second set of pitches that are related because they are NOT in that chord! Then, is it not logical to assume that because BOTH sets of pitches are connected to the same chord – in a way – the TOTALITY of the two sets consists of a further, equally valid relationship?

"Whoa! Hold on there, please! This is getting a little complicated! We were writing etudes to explore the potential of various CHORD TONES, and then we were writing etudes to explore the potential of SUB TONES, and we discovered all kinds of interesting creative pathways in both groups. Now you're saying we are supposed to somehow fold the two groups into each other? I don't get it!"

Such a reaction is not surprising. The theory of Modus Lascivus has expanded musical creative potential to such an extent within its basic organization it's difficult to see how it could go still further, but this new step is simply a logical extension of what we have investigated thus far.

The governing theory is very simple: If membership in a given structure creates a relationship within the "member pitches", then membership OUTSIDE that same structure creates an equally valid relationship as well. So, if the chord-tones are related, and the sub-tones are related, then the two groups must be related as well, as they all derive from the same original structure!

The "wise theorist" (as in "Aesop's Musical Fables") now states, "*Aha! If all twelve pitches are thus related, then you are saying the entire chromatic scale is one single "structure", and therefore there IS no structure – just variations amongst the twelve tones. Hence you are validating the TWELVE-TONE SYSTEM – the very one you decried earlier!*" But the "wise author" answers thus: "*No, you have misinterpreted what I wrote. While all twelve pitches are involved when the two elements are combined, they MAINTAIN THEIR MODUS INDIVIDUALITY AT ALL TIMES so that the two groups of any 'collection' remain as separate entities throughout a composition.*"

Obviously, this needs a little clarification: There are eighty-two structures in Modus Lascivus. Each structure has a unique set of chord-tones, and therefore a unique set of subsidiary-tones. That means that for each "chord" the chromatic scale is subdivided differently, and that "difference" provides the exceptional creative potential inherent to Modus. In other words, as you will see below, there are several ways of incorporating the two sets of pitches in a given composition, but in every case the objective is to maintain the separate "family identities" of each set throughout. It is this very "sub-organization" that creates not only the "freshness" of music in Modus but maintains a FUNDAMENTAL THEORETICAL LOGIC that makes the "new music" work as well as the "old music".

In a way, this concept could be considered a reflection of the device in conventional music where a composer MODULATES from one key to another – the same twelve pitches are employed in both keys, but now in a totally new relationship. The main point here is that when writing in Modus Lascivus, all twelve tones should remain "organized" and "separately-assigned" (chord tones or sub tones) throughout the composition.

There are several ways of "combining" chord-tones and sub-tones in a single work, and it behooves you to create a few more etudes employing the options listed below to familiarize yourself with the resulting SOUND of each approach. That is the ideal way for you to personally "hear" how the two groups relate on this larger scale.

The options are as follows:

1. "HARMONIC" CONVERGENCE

You have already written etudes with just chord-tones and just sub-tones. Now choose any structure and create a short piece with the two "families" separated "harmonically" – that is, place one family of notes ABOVE, and the other BELOW. Since you now have twelve tones with which to work, you can choose which notes you want to sound with which other notes, but it's important to maintain that vertical separation whenever possible.

If the above seems confusing, let us demonstrate how this technique of harmonic or vertical "integration" works in practical usage. Figure 33 on the following page is a condensed score of an excerpt from the author's first large-scale attempt to compose in Modus Lascivus – the first movement of a three-movement symphony. The excerpt's inclusion is in no way meant to impress the reader with the author's compositional skills (or lack thereof) – it is presented solely to offer one example of this particular horizontal application (one group of tones over or under the other) in a "real" piece of music.

The first movement of the symphony (Figure 33 excerpt) was specifically designed so that the CHORD-TONES (Chord III-4, the C Diminished Triad shown in Figure 32) are relegated strictly to the lowest instruments, and the NINE SUBSIDIARY TONES of Chord III-4 are all set above them.

Figure 32

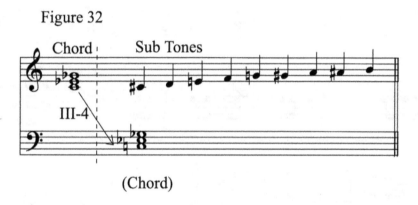

(Chord)

As should be apparent in the short example of Figure 33 that follows, the symphony was purposely focused on conventional pitch relationships (it begins and ends solidly in the "Key of C") to demonstrate how familiar sounds can be extracted from what appears to be a complex tonal organization.

As you view the score, you should once again note that ENHARMONICISM plays a major role in establishing those relationships, and once again, yet again, let it be restated that this excerpt is not presented for "objective evaluation of the author's compositional skills" – it is included only to allow the reader to absorb how these combinations of chord- and sub-tones SOUND by actually **PLAYING** them.

As described above (Figure 32), the three "Chord Tones" of the C Diminished Triad are on the "bottom" (stems down), and the "Sub Tones" are on top.

Figure 33   Bilik: "Symphony ML", 1st Movement (excerpt)

Naturally, if one chooses to employ this vertical or "harmonic" convergence, it is equally feasible to create a piece with the chord-tones on top and the subsidiary tones below – it makes no difference musically. It just depends upon what you, as the creator want to project in terms of tonalities and sonorities. The potential is literally unlimited.

2. MELODIC CONVERGENCE

In this case, the idea is that, instead of placing one set of tones above or below the other within your composition, you ALTERNATE the two groups of pitches across the full tonal spectrum, employing first one set of tones and <u>then</u> the other. You can alternate every beat, every measure, every phrase, or in whatever "lengths" you want.

This concept works most easily with the six-note structures (for the obvious reason of an equal division) but can be accomplished with any of the eighty-two chords. The results of this technique are most unusual and intriguing melodic and harmonic "progressions" as the music veers back and forth from one set of pitches to the other.

Again, using the author's symphony as an example (not because it's so "good", but because it's easy to analyze!), the <u>second</u> movement employs that exact approach – alternating between six-note chord-tones and sub-tones – first, in half-measure increments, then in single-measure increments, and later in larger increments (see Figure 35, below). In terms of the SOUND (the most important element in Modus), the alternation is virtually undetectable as such unless one is specifically listening for it. Upon hearing the music, it appears to be just a gentle, soft "elegy", but in actuality is nothing more than an experimental expanded "etude" on Chord VI-3, as shown below in Figure 34!

Figure 34

By carefully examining the two groups above and noticing which pitches belong to which group (keep "enharmonics" in mind!), you should be able to easily discern how the "alternation" proceeds in the following excerpt (Figure 35). Once again, the point of including these samples is simply to establish how these basically consonant sonorities sound to YOU, and THAT can only be achieved by **PLAYING** them.

Figure 35   Bilik;   "Symphony ML", Second Movement (excerpt)
                            (VI-3)

As stated above, this "melodic alternating" technique is most easily accomplished using the six-note chords since the two sets of tones contain equal pitch-potential, but by no means does one need to be limited to that particular rank. The lesson here is how the common "ancestry" of <u>all</u> the notes allows them to function so smoothly whether one chooses to imply conventional tonality or not.

3. COMBINED MODES

To qualify for your "Graduate Degree in Modus Lascivus" (!!!), once you have completed a few etudes in the previous formats, you can and should experiment with new and different ways of combining those concepts. You can alternate and switch the sub-tones and chord-tones with their opposites by moving them above or below each other, or you can alternate the two groups melodically in some lines while constructing vertical relationships with others. If that sounds confusing, all it means is that in this creative mode, as long as you maintain the "adhesion" of each particular group of tones, you can basically do ANTYTHING!

One hopes by this point you can begin to grasp the full creative potential of Modus Lascivus. The only "caveat" to complete understanding is trying to remain "true" to the basic organization of pitches as much as possible (keeping each group together). Of course, you won't go to jail if you "cheat" now and then and sneak in an "alien" note for expressive purposes (as the author has done in a few instances), but just as there were "conventions" when writing in the "old style", following the basic precepts of Modus will definitely result in a more logical and solid foundation for whatever you create.

For those readers with a higher threshold of pain who might be interested in hearing and examining ALL of the author's "Symphony", it might be possible to locate a recording online such as through YouTube or other sources, and a complete full score of the concert-band version is available for purchase from Excelcia Music Publishing or from other retail music dealers.

Should you thus persevere, in the third movement of the work you will hear (and see) how the pitches wander into this more complex intermingling of combinations, at times chord-tones are voiced in the "center" of the music with sub-tones surrounding them both above and below, while at other times the piece is actually in THREE KEYS AT ONCE! Yet, to the listener, everything still sounds relatively "normal" because (of course) all the pitches are related via the basic chord employed, which, in the third movement happens to be Chord VI-5 (you can find it on the chart in Appendix 1).

To summarize these past chapters, the compositional options within Modus Lascivus are so vast, it is pointless to try and point out all the minor details of its application. Ultimately, how and when you use Modus will be up to YOU or whomever you may be guiding. The ideal way of exploiting the "system" is to select some chord and first "fool around" creatively with the chord tones themselves – what is their melodic potential? What is their harmonic potential? Then you should investigate the same elements of that chord's subsidiary tones, and THEN you begin experimenting with alternating the two groups or putting one on top of the other as described previously.

The complexity of all this new information is likely rather mind-boggling, BUT... the payoff is that what you or your cohort create – no matter the style and no matter how "modern" or how "conventional" – it will possess an inherent theoretical logic that binds the sounds into a unified whole – the very thing missing in the vast majority of contemporary music today. In most new "serious" music, in "modern jazz", in "Hip-Hop", in "country", in so many categories, it is the absence of "fundamental tonal logic" and/or "effective artistic creativity" that keeps works from attaining the powerful emotional reactions achieved by composers (classical and popular) of the past.

Way back in the 1920s and 30s George Gershwin had the courage to embark on a revolutionary quest to bring the music of jazz and the blues into the classical arena, and the works he produced proved that with consummate skill and daring one could accomplish the unimaginable – works of a hybrid language never heard before, and seldom equaled since. Gershwin succeeded admirably, so is it not possible YOU might succeed as well? Why not!

CHAPTER FOURTEEN - "NOW WHAT ?"

The preceding chapters have been devoted to the presentation of Tibor Serly's contemporary music theory – a theory that could serve as a springboard for the creation of new, effective works in all possible styles. But Modus Lascivus is only a THEORY – it is just a template for logically organizing the twelve tones in various combinations based on sound harmonic and acoustical principles. Just because a "student" of Modus might write some clever little etudes utilizing various elements of the theory does not guarantee the production of a "masterwork" or a "mega-hit". There is another element involved that goes far beyond simple "ditties" and mastering THAT is no easy task.

To understand this, you, gentle reader, whether a budding composer or a "mentor" to one, must "play the part" of a MUSIC LISTENER and for the moment forget all other elements involved in music-making. Close your eyes (well, don't do THAT or you won't be able to read what follows!) and think about one single piece of music you might select if you were to be alone for a long, long time, and could only have one CD or music file (and a player) with you. OK? Done? Good!

Now, think about that piece. Obviously, if you chose it, you are "hearing" it, or parts of it, in your "inner ear", and whatever you're "hearing" must be the source of some sort of positive feeling (or you wouldn't have chosen it!). Now, try to "unwind time" a little and think backwards to how the music you selected was first CREATED. Somebody "heard" that same music in THEIR inner ear before it was ever played and decided that the pattern of pitches was worth "working on". How that "attractive theme" <u>was</u> "worked on" is the factor that separates the wheat from the chaff in this most unusual art.

As you listen to any piece of music, your brain is responding to a sequence of sounds, and that sequence either appeals to you (creates some kind of positive response inside your head), or just passes through in the manner of "background noise". While you may not have responded to the latter version, somebody else must have thought that sequence of sounds was "pretty good" or they wouldn't have taken the time and trouble to write it down in the first place.

And now we come to the absolute crux of music: The WRITER may think what they're creating is just wonderful (obviously, or why bother to make the effort), but the TRUE TEST is what the LISTENER thinks. Whether an ambitious classical composition or a jazz, country, pop, or rock tune, the "secret of success" lies in how the original musical idea is "fashioned" in terms of maintaining the listener's interest for the length of TIME the piece consumes, or even better, getting the listener involved in the music EMOTIONALLY. A writer may "hear" some really effective musical pattern, but ultimate success lies in how he or she manipulates those pitches IN THE MEDIUM OF TIME to create something that literally "resonates" with the listener.

Mastery of musical "time control", whether a long-form or short piece, is based on specific skills, and sadly, while Modus Lascivus is tremendously useful in discovering new and effective pitch relationships, what to DO with those pitches involves learning and mastering compositional techniques exhibited by previous masters, regardless of "style".

In other words, for any composer or arranger, regardless of how "inspired" a specific idea may be, it can't become a great success if that person doesn't know what to do with that "kernel of inspiration" for the next minute, or ten minutes, or thirty minutes. That's where an experienced teacher or mentor comes in – someone who might guide a creative person in "fleshing out" original ideas. The "secret" of any successful musical endeavor is how the sounds are aligned to first pique the listener's interest and then what must be done to MAINTAIN it. Whether employing Modus or not, the principles are pretty well-established.

As stated in an earlier chapter, the best "hook" to "catch" the listener is some form of MELODY or melodic motif – some sequence of pitches that is easily embedded in the listener's mind. Once established, the "good composer" uses those same pitches (or more accurately that same SEQUENCE OF INTERVALS, since starting points may get moved up or down as the piece goes on) to create various "shapes" and "structures". This refers to devices such as "sequences" (ascending or descending repetitions of a motif), rhythmic alteration (condensing or expanding the motif), modulating the motif (presenting it in different modes or tonal-centers), "imitating" the motif (using counterpoint), and varying the "color" of the motif via clever orchestration.

Of course, the above represents just the first elementary stage of successful composition – the real skill comes from "the big picture" – how a writer puts all the "tricks" together to create a satisfying "journey" for the listener. The longer a composition, the more important it is to create a perceptible structure or form – some kind of "aural shape" that the listener's inner ear can follow. As that shape (of course invisible and only existing in TIME) becomes evident and eventually works itself to a satisfactory conclusion, it then successfully "wraps up" the experience for the listener, and hopefully he or she feels the devotion of time proved worthwhile.

To be absolutely clear, the attention to detail described above applies equally to "popular" works as well as to "serious" ones. Just go back one more time and review the recordings of "Bolero" and "Over the Rainbow" and you will hear precisely how the "form" and "structure" (the overall shape) of each play such a dominant role. For that matter, you can review any composition you personally happen to enjoy hearing and pay attention to its overall shape. THAT criteria should be the objective of any creative musical endeavor.

Depending on your own prior experience in composing (or coaching composers), if you feel any lack of confidence in being able to achieve the desired creative goals, the wisest course of action BY FAR is to do some intensive research and locate an accomplished writer, performer, or teacher familiar with your chosen musical style with whom you might sit down (or meet "remotely") and analyze successful various works (by that person or others) to determine exactly why they are "good" – why they seem to "work". However you engage in these sessions, this is a crucial step in the quest to go beyond producing some random "cool sounds" and instead gaining an understanding of what it takes to make a musical endeavor truly outstanding.

If, on the other hand, you feel capable of clinically analyzing other's music on your own, the next step at this point would be to identify three or four pieces in your favorite style that strike you as the "ultimate examples" – the best of the best in that style – and sit yourself down and listen to each several times, paying attention to exactly HOW and WHY the piece works for you. Focus specifically on the shape of "melodies", on any effective harmonic progressions, on rhythmic patterns that "catch on", on the overall "shape" or "contour" of the piece, and in particular on how a tonal center is established – IF one is established.

Let me repeat once again: The ideas presented in this text lay out a theoretical concept that provides a new and logically-based language for combining the twelve tones of the chromatic scale, but incorporating those concepts into an actual composition requires an entirely different set of skills – skills and knowledge that involve learning how best to SEQUENCE and ORGANIZE pitches to form a satisfactory and appealing SHAPE that most listeners would find appealing. If, as a writer, you are familiar with those techniques, then by all means "go for it", but, if not, it behooves you to find someone who IS, and learn as much as you can from what they have to offer. In that endeavor, best of luck!

CHAPTER FIFTEEN - "SELF-COMPOSED"

In this final chapter, we will conclude our exploration of Modus Lascivus with one concrete example of how its organizational principles might be applied to "real" music. The idea is that by experiencing an actual public performance of a composition conceived entirely on Modus principles, along with viewing the score itself, you will be better able to make the transition from the "theoretical" side to how it works in practice. Hopefully, this will be the step that leads you to more fully understand and embrace this exciting new musical language of today.

Believe it or not, it is possible to find numerous examples of "serious" music in which composers have instinctively drifted into the concepts of Modus without realizing it. If one listens carefully or analyzes the scores of certain works by Stravinsky, Bartók, or Gershwin, or even further back to those of Chopin, Debussy, and Ravel, you will notice that in place of conventional "tonal" devices (harmonic sequences such as "V to I" and common resolutions of leading-tones), they often incorporate MODAL RELATIONSHIPS with notes organized according to a certain "color" or "feel" and resolutions of "tension" coming from other harmonic intervals. On close examination, it is possible to perceive those "modes" as being related to specific vertical structures, but parsing such relationships is difficult and is probably best left to those truly interested in advanced music theory!

Similarly, in jazz, rock, and other "popular" styles – even Hip-Hop – one finds a majority of examples where the harmonic relationships are NOT those of conventional tonal music, but more often modal in character. This is particularly true of the musical language of the "Blues", in which the harmonic progression incorporates the SUB-DOMINANT harmonies far more frequently than the conventional dominant ones. If all of this doesn't make much sense to you, that's OK – the point is there are numerous examples of great music in every style instinctively exploiting the same principles delineated by Serly in his theory.

To allow you to hear and see for yourself what a CONSCIOUS APPLICATION of Modus Lascivus "sounds like", as the final effort in this endeavor, an original composition by the author has been included in Appendix 2, but **let us be perfectly clear:** this is in no way meant to "display awesome creative skills" or to imply that this is some great piece of music to go down in the annals of history – it is NOT! It is included only because the composition was created specifically for the purpose of demonstrating "Modus" in a true concert format.

In essence, the work is simply a collection of expanded "etudes" originally written to explore the creative potential of various chordal structures but reworked to form a large-scale composition. The objective of the composer (that's me) was to create the most "accessible" (consonant) product possible rather than revel in creative extremes of dissonance. This was done consciously to illustrate how the new system can serve as an equally creative source for the most "ordinary" conventional harmonic and tonal practices and yet sound somehow new and different.

As a result, the composition that follows sounds very "tonal" despite the fact that there is not a single conventional harmonic progression such as "V to I". Each movement is constructed in a strict standard compositional form for the same reason: to tie Tibor Serly's concept all the way back to the original fundamental theory of Jean Phillipe Rameau. Even the selection of the most conventional concert ensemble as the medium of performance – the String Quartet – was part of the plan to bring Serly's theory solidly into the mainstream.

The result is a quartet (two violins, viola, and cello) divided into four movements:

I.   Theme and Variations
II. Scherzo and Trio
III. Song Form (A-B-A)
IV. Rondo (but in a unique form called "Rondo Cancrizan" or "Crab Rondo" – a classical form in which half-way through, the music suddenly goes exactly BACKWARDS towards the beginning – a device particularly appropriate to demonstrate the potential of Modus Lascivus!)

To fully absorb the objective of this example of Modus writing, it is strongly suggested you follow the procedure outlined below exactly as shown, as that will implant the principles in your "ear" as well as in your "thinking center" as efficiently as possible.

1. Go online, and access YouTube. Type in "JERRY BILIK STRING QUARTET", and "String Quartet in Modus Lascivus" should appear.

2. Get a warm or a cool "libation", sit back, and just soak in the performance. And again, let us be crystal clear about the objective: You are NOT supposed to decide if this is a "good piece" or a "bad piece" or a "mediocre piece". You are supposed to just absorb the sounds, to get a sense of the modal colors involved in each movement, because, as you'll come to realize, Modus produces a palette that sounds both familiar and "not-so-familiar" at the same time, and THAT is what the inclusion of this performance is trying to implant in your mind.

3. Once you have listened to the entire quartet, the next step is to come back to this text and carefully review the following "Modus Explanation" of each of the four movements. To fully comprehend these explanations, you should compare the notes below to the actual quartet score (see Appendix 2). This is the most critical moment, as it allows you to coordinate the text, the written notes, and the actual SOUND of what you heard (and which of course you can hear again at any time by re-accessing the YouTube version!). As you will discover, from time to time the composer has added "irregular notes" (those not in a particular "group") for purely artistic purposes, and as there exists no "Modus Lascivus Police Force", one composing in this system can of course feel free to "break the rules" when the muse so suggests!

4. Once you feel you have gained some understanding of the structure of each movement, go back once again and play the quartet on YouTube, but this time, ignore the video and just concentrate on studying the score as the performance plays. This is how you make the final mental connection between what is written and what you hear, and this is the moment (hopefully) when everything that has preceded this point in the exposition of Modus Lascivus becomes clear. This is also the moment that the full import of ENHARMONICISM becomes evident!

So, to review…

STEP ONE: Locate "Jerry Bilik String Quartet" on YouTube.

STEP TWO: Sit yourself down, get comfortable, and listen to the performance without perusing any additional material. For this "assignment" to work properly in terms of "cementing" the Modus principles in your mind, you should really follow these instructions as precisely as possible (not that there's anything anyone can do about it if you don't!), as this whole endeavor is all about properly absorbing what needs to be absorbed!

STEP THREE: If you have done as requested and viewed the actual performance, now you have earned the right to proceed! (Continue to following page!)

THEORETICAL ANALYSIS

STRING QUARTET IN MODUS LASCIVUS

(listed on YouTube as "Jerry Bilik – String Quartet")

MOVEMENT I. "VARIATIONS"

Figure 36

VI-15

INTRODUCTION	(m. 1–20)	SUB-TONES ONLY
TRANSITION & THEME	(m. 21–39)	CHORD-TONES ONLY
VARIATION I	(m. 40–60)	CHORD-TONES on top, SUB-TONES on bottom
VARIATIONS II & III	(m. 61–101)	SUB-TONES (plus some "exceptions")
VARIATION IV	(m. 101–121)	CHORD-TONES ONLY
VARIATION V, PT. 1	(m. 122–127)	SUB-TONES ONLY
VARIATION V, PT. 2	(m. 128–149)	ALTERNATING GROUPS (CHORD, SUB, ETC.)
VARIATION VI	(m. 150–158)	CHORD-TONES in the middle, SUB-TONES top & bottom
CODA, PART 1	(m. 159–162)	CHORD-TONES below, SUB-TONES above
CODA, PART 2	(m. 162–end)	SUB-TONES ONLY

Figure 37

VII-21

MOVEMENT II. "SCHERZO"

INTRO & "A" THEME	(m. 1–26)	CHORD-TONES ONLY
TRANSITION	(m. 27–35)	CHORD-TONES and SUB-TONES MIXED
"A" THEME AGAIN	(m. 35–74)	CHORD-TONES ONLY (some SUB TONES near end)
TRIO	(m. 75–104)	SUB-TONES above, CHORD-TONES below
"A" THEME, TRANS.	(m. 105–127)	CHORD-TONES and SUB-TONES MIXED
CODA ("A" THEME)	(m. 128–end)	CHORD-TONES ONLY

MOVEMENT III. "ELEGY"

NOTE: Unlike the first two movements, the Third Movement employs two DIFFERENT seven-note structures. To help with the analysis, the segments of the movement have been broken down according to which seven-note chord is "in play" rather than in the order in which they occur. Thus, the final "A" section (Part 3) is listed under the opening section, since both employ the same chordal structure.

"A" SEGMENTS:

Figure 38

VII-26

| "A", PART 1 | (m. 1–41) | CHORD-TONES above, SUB-TONES below (some variations) |
| "A", PART 3 | (m. 93–end) | CHORD-TONES above, SUB-TONES below (like "A", PART 1) |

"A", PART 2 and "B" SEGMENTS:

Figure 39

VII-10

"A", PART 2	(m. 42–70)	CHORD-TONES ONLY (some variation)
TRANSITION	(m. 71–81)	CHORD-TONES, SUB-TONES, ALTERNATING
"B", PART 2	(m. 82–93)	CHORD-TONES ONLY (like "A", PART 2)

MOVEMENT IV. "RONDO CANCRIZAN"

NOTE: As mentioned earlier, this movement follows the traditional Rondo format, but halfway through, after the "climax" (at m. 114–118), the notes appear in the exact reverse order as they were first introduced (with a slight modification in the final "backwards" B-Section) until the piece concludes with a short "Coda" commencing in m. 217. It is also interesting to note that although the seven-note structure is built from the root "C" (as explained earlier), the tones naturally gravitate towards a "home base" of "E".

Figure 40

VI-3

INTRODUCTION	(m. 1–17)	CHORD-TONES ONLY (some variation)
"A" THEME	(m. 18–41)	CHORD-TONES ONLY
"B" SECTION, PART 1	(m. 42–52)	CHORD-TONES center, SUB-TONES surrounding
"B" SECTION, PART 2	(m. 53–67)	CHORD-TONES above, SUB-TONES below (var.)
"A" THEME RETURN	(m. 68–92)	CHORD-TONES ONLY
"C" SECTION, PART 1	(m. 93–98)	CHORD-TONES center, SUB-TONES surrounding
"C" SECTION, PART 2	(m. 99–114)	CHORD-TONES below, SUB-TONES above
CLIMAX	(m. 114–118)	CLUSTER CHORD, MIXED PITCHES

[REVERSE:]

"C" SECTION, PART 3	(m. 119–133)	CHORD-TONES below, SUB-TONES above
"C" SECTION, PART 4	(m. 134–140)	CHORD-TONES center, SUB-TONES surrounding
"A" THEME RETURN	(m. 141–164)	CHORD-TONES ONLY
"B" SECTION, PART 3	(m. 164–168)	CHORD-TONES center, SUB-TONES surrounding
"B" SECTION, PART 4	(m. 169–178)	CHORD-TONES above, SUB-TONES below
"B" SECTION, PART 5	(m. 179–188)	CHORD-TONES center, SUB-TONES surrounding
"A" THEME RETURN	(m. 189–212)	CHORD-TONES ONLY
CODA	(m. 213–end)	CHORD-TONES & SUB-TONES alternating & mixing

After reviewing the outline above and cross-checking it with the full score (included in Appendix 2), it is recommended that the reader re-play the entire quartet on YouTube but focus strictly on the <u>score</u> rather than the video to implant the relationships between what is notated and what is heard.

FINAL NOTE: The original goal in the creation of this string quartet was to have the "normal" (unenlightened!) listener (and performers) focus solely on the MUSIC and not on the underlying Modus Lascivus construction. That objective, which should be the goal of any new work so constructed, is to substantiate the practical value of Tibor Serly's theory – that a composer can adapt it to his or her own musical tastes and concentrate on making effective pieces, knowing that there is a sound THEORY behind this particular approach.

C O D A

If you, dear reader, have no problem with the state of today's music in your chosen style, then it's likely this experience has proven of little value, and for that the author apologizes profusely. If, however, you feel that new "great works" in your particular "language" are few and far between, perhaps you, or another writer with whom you're familiar, might seriously consider this new creative process in which one selects related pitches arising from this new vertical-to-horizontal concept (just as you did in your "etudes") and see where your imagination might take you (or them).

The primary goal of this book is an attempt to validate the conventional harmonic concepts put forth by Rameau so many years ago – a validation supported by the vast library of works (classical, popular, jazz, R & B, etc.) that have proven so effective within that conventional idiom. What Tibor Serly has done in creating Modus Lascivus was to uncover the most logical and practical theory for E X P A N D I N G the basic harmonic principles of "yore", and in so doing revealed all kinds of pitch relationships which can be exploited to give a fresh and exciting "feel" to new music of all types.

One further important point in all of this is for you, dear reader, to realize that this isn't "Beginning Music Theory 101". There are no "rules" that say you MUST stay strictly within given groupings of pitches – Heaven forbid! The value of Modus is providing you, the writer, with an aural guide as to how certain chosen pitches engender a kind of "familial relationship" – they just seem to "go together better", and that makes whatever you write within that relationship more "comfortable" for the listener. Regardless of what some people might suggest, in music, it IS all about the LISTENER. If a piece doesn't "register" with a "hearer", the writer can brag and boast all they want about how clever they are, but the only true "test" is whether or not someone will put up their "dough-re-me" to hear someone else's "do-re-mi".

Now, whether writer, arranger, teacher, critic, or just "official listener", you're on your own. If amongst the former and you know of a good mentor or coach, hopefully they will guide you to study the "Big Hits" in your chosen style – to discern WHY a certain piece works – and the more you can absorb those clues, the sooner you'll be able to produce other "works that work". To this end, it is the author's sincerest hope that this book might in some way be of help.

As stated before... Good luck to us both!

APPENDIX 1

MODUS LASCIVUS VERTICAL (CHORD) STRUCTRUES

MAJOR CHORDS

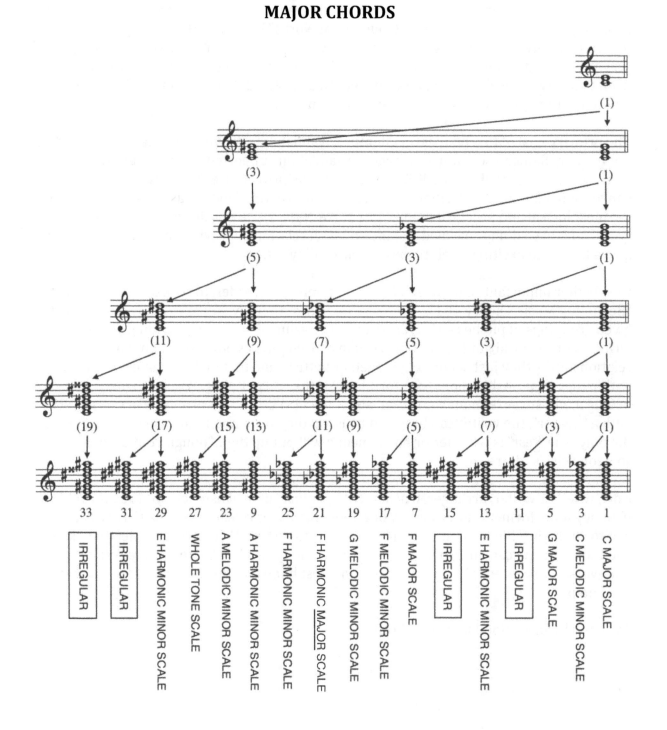

APPENDIX 1 (CONTINUED)

MODUS LASCIVUS VERTICAL (CHORD) STRUCTRUES

MINOR CHORDS

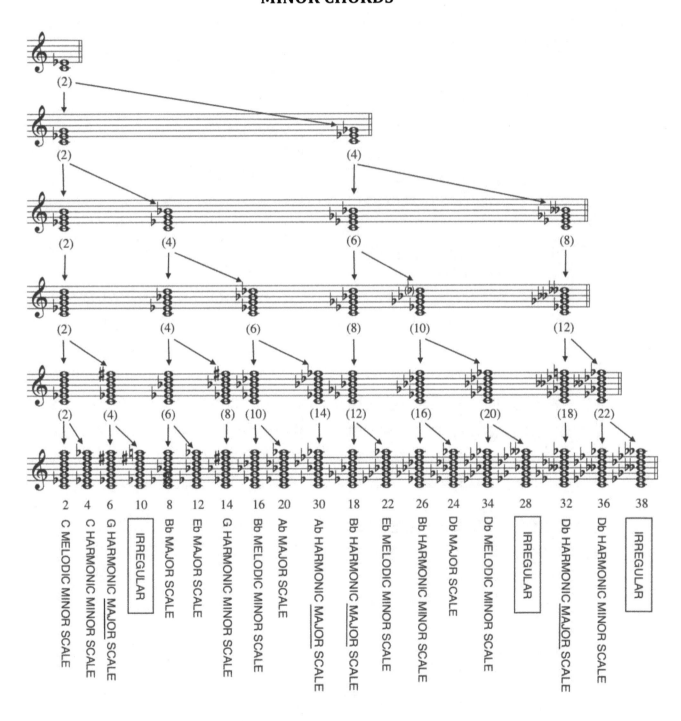

APPENDIX 2

STRING QUARTET *in Modus Lascivus*

By JERRY H. BILIK

I. VARIATIONS

© 2012 Jerry Bilik Music, Inc.

78

II. SCHERZO

III. ELEGY

IV. RONDO CANCRIZAN

Allegro con spirito (♩ = 128)

-33- *STRING QUARTET in Modus Lascivus*

-34- *STRING QUARTET in Modus Lascivus*

Piu Mosso

-35- *STRING QUARTET in Modus Lascivus*

-36- *STRING QUARTET in Modus Lascivus*

APPENDIX 3

Dedication Note from Tibor Serly from the First Edition of his "Modus Lascivus"

In 1976, with the help of his "students", Tibor Serly published a book describing Modus Lascivus. Despite our best efforts to assist him, the result proved too esoteric for most readers, and it fell into disuse. This present effort is an attempt to reincarnate Serly's work.

> ML No. 2, is for Jerry Belik
> and who deserves it more ?.
>
> for 1) your confidence from beginning to ML's completion,
>
> 2) your Contribution — more correctly — Collaboration
>
> 3) your never faltering loyalty
>
> 4) What else can one say!
>
> With many Thanks
> Your teacher, friend and colleague
> Tibor   Sept. 1976
>
> (Tibor Serly)

On October 8th, 1978, Tibor Serly was fatally struck by a London City Bus while on his way to receiving a Medal of the State from his native Hungary in recognition of his great talent and contribution to the art of music.

jerrybilikmusic.com

Printed in the USA
CPSIA information can be obtained
at www.ICGtesting.com
LVHW081326181223
766618LV00008B/833